S0-AVO-300

THE MIDDLE EAST
AND NORTH AFRICA

The Middle East and North Africa

THE CHALLENGE TO WESTERN SECURITY

Peter Duignan
L. H. Gann

HOOVER INSTITUTION PRESS
Stanford University, Stanford, California

*The Hoover Institution on War, Revolution and Peace, founded at
Stanford University in 1919 by the late President Herbert Hoover,
is an interdisciplinary research center for advanced study on
domestic and international affairs in the twentieth century. The views
expressed in its publications are entirely those of the authors
and do not necessarily reflect the views of the staff, officers,
or Board of Overseers of the Hoover Institution.*

Hoover Press Publication 239

©1981 by the Board of Trustees of the
Leland Stanford Junior University
All rights reserved
International Standard Book Number: 0-8179-7392-3
Library of Congress Catalog Card Number: 80-82749
Printed in the United States of America
Second printing, 1983
Design by Elizabeth Gehman

CONTENTS

FIGURES

PREFACE

The Middle East comprises a great landmass stretching from the Atlantic shore of Morocco to the mountains of Iran. This great region is of major importance to world culture by reason of the skills, abilities, and achievements of its inhabitants. The Middle East has been a font of Western civilization. From the Middle East derive the three great monotheistic religions of mankind—Judaism, Christianity, and Islam. The Middle East is also of great significance to Western defense as a result of its strategic location and its natural resources, especially oil.

The Middle East is split into a variety of states of unequal size, power, and economic attainments. These states possess little political cohesion; conflicts between them are often paralleled by clashes between ethnic groups within individual states. The predominance of communal loyalties frequently weakens national cohesion and works against political compromise. With the exception of Israel and Turkey, the Middle Eastern governments are authoritarian in form, being mostly based on the rule of a single dominant party or the military.

The political problems of the Middle East are widely paralleled by economic difficulties of staggering proportions. In most countries, except in a few socioeconomic "islands" like Israel, the birth rate remains high; urbanization is rapid; unemployment and illiteracy are wide spread. More and more youngsters leave the villages or the desert in order to find jobs in what appears to them to be a more interesting and challenging way of life in the cities. Mass unemployment, especially in societies with a high proportion of young men and women, makes for political radicalism, although not necessarily of a Marxist type.

The cultures of the Middle East, since the seventh century, have been shaped largely by the religion of Islam, which can lend itself to revolutionary advance, as well as to staunch conservatism. But whatever its origin, radicalism in the Middle East looks for rapid solutions, enforced, if necessary, by gelignite or guns. Radicalism in turn often spills over into foreign policy; subversive activities in a neighbor's territory or plots to overthrow a hostile government are widely regarded as legitimate forms of diplomatic endeavor.

The last thirty years have seen vast economic changes in the Middle East. New industries have grown up; cities have expanded; agricultural methods have sometimes improved. Standards of farming vary from excellent to poor, but the greater part of the agriculturists still employ backward methods. Their enterprise is widely impeded by a lack of markets, transport, capital investments, technological know-how, or sometimes, by mistaken application of agricultural technology resulting in injury to the environment. The farmer's lot is often worsened by natural obstacles placed in the way of prosperity— droughts, floods, locusts, and cattle and plant diseases. Unfortunately, many governments pay insufficient attention to the farmer's needs. The bulk of investment has gone into industry (including prestige projects of a kind that poor countries cannot afford) and the armed forces. Cumbrous, inefficient, and overmanned bureaucracies act as a brake on development while consuming much of the taxpayer's money.

In spite of these troubles, Middle Eastern countries have made striking advances. Nothing would be more mistaken than to underestimate their resilience and ingenuity. Nevertheless, no magic formula has been devised that will cope with the multifarious problems caused by lack of resources, agricultural underdevelopment, rapid urbanization, and a high birth rate. Successful modernization, insofar as it is likely to come, should be of an incremental sort—cautious and slow. By and large, we do not anticipate quick and spectacular development; we anticipate a decade of difficulties and strife, punctuated perhaps by some slow but genuine achievements.

Before the outbreak of World War II, United States interests in the Middle East were mainly of an economic kind; American entrepreneurs and technicians, like British ones, took a major part in creating the Middle Eastern oil industries. The balance of political power lay with Great Britain and France. As World War II ended, British predominance still seemed secure. The British had played the leading military part in that theater; in Syria and Lebanon, Lybia and Ethiopia, British intervention had won local independence from France and Italy. The British strength was more apparent than real; finally, they withdrew from Palestine and from the Suez Canal Zone. Growing Soviet pressure then induced the Americans to take a more active part in the Middle East. The failure of Franco-British military intervention in Suez in 1956 marked a diplomatic revolution; the United States became the predominant Western power in the region and the Middle East became a major concern of American policy makers.

The present book, a companion volume to our study, *Africa South of the Sahara: The Challenge to Western Security*, grew out of a major project initiated by the Hoover Institution, of which *The United States in the 1980s* (edited by Peter Duignan and Alvin Rabushka, 1980), is the keynote volume. We look at the Middle East from the standpoint of American vital interests. We provide a general introduction designed to do away with some widespread stereotypes concerning Islam. We then deal with a number of specific themes—political, economic, and social—that transcend the problems of individual countries. We pass on to regional trouble spots—the Maghreb, Israel and its neighbors, Lebanon, Iran, the Persian Gulf, Saudi Arabia, and Turkey. We conclude with a discussion of Soviet involvement in the area, and of special American interests as affected by the related problems of energy and Soviet expansion.

We write for the general reader rather than for specialists. We make policy recommendations, and we analyze the area's problems and prospects. In outlining our proposals, we have tried to set the Middle East in the wider framework of world politics and super-power competition. Our approach unashamedly takes as its starting point United States national interests. Our treatment will not convince those who regard international politics as an exercise in higher morality according to which American national conerns should be subordinate to those of other nations, or disregarded altogether in favor of trilateralism or some similar design.

In reaching our conclusions, we have tried to take Soviet opinion makers, Soviet military strategists, and Soviet party politicians at their own valuation. According to Soviet thinkers, peaceful coexistence and détente are but instruments in an international class struggle in which there can be no compromise, in which there can be only victors and vanquished. The winners of this conflict will be the Communists; the losers will be the Western democracies. The rulers of the USSR regard foreign policy as war by other than military means; war is revolution by other means; revolution implies the ascendancy of a "new class" of party functionaries and ideologues whose power will ultimately cement the supremacy of the Soviet Union in the Middle East—and in the world at large.

We should like to thank those who have read our manuscript, especially John Devlin of Washington, DC, and L. Carl Brown of Princeton University. Their willingness to peruse this text does not, of course, necessarily indicate agreement with our views.

PETER DUIGNAN
L. H. GANN

Stanford, California

The World of Islam

The Muslim world spans half the globe. It reaches from Morocco to Egypt, from the Muslim enclaves of southeastern Europe to the southern frontier of Islam in sub-Saharan Africa, from the shores of the Mediterranean to the mountains of Afghanistan—and far beyond, to the Indian subcontinent, to Indonesia and the Philippines. Only about one-third of the world's Muslims live in the Middle East, a huge and ill-defined land mass.

Definitions of the Middle East vary considerably. The most comprehensive one likens the Middle East to a giant eagle. The bird's main body consists of Egypt and the Nile valley, including the Sudan. The eastern wing is formed by the Muslim portion of Asia, which extends from the southern shore of the Mediterranean to the peaks of Afghanistan in the northeast and the Indian Ocean in the east. The remainder of North Africa, from Lybia all the way to Morocco and Mauritania, makes up its western wing. The Middle East, in other words, does not lie in the east. Morocco is no farther from the United States than Great Britain; Egypt is no more distant from our shores than Finland.

The Middle Eastern landmass shows great variation in its geographic structure and scenery. All Middle Eastern countries, however, have one feature in common: much of their surface lacks water. Geographers estimate that about 99 percent of Saudi Arabia, 97 percent of Egypt, 70 percent of Iraq, and 50 percent of Syria is covered by dry steppes and desert. Fiction associates the desert with endless sand dunes where mounted bedouins lurk in ambush. Sandy wastes do indeed extend over enormous areas, as do pebbled or gravel deserts and rocky wastelands—perhaps the world's most desolate and forbidding scenery. But large desert areas are not bare of vegetation. Where seasonal rainfall is available, pastoralists can make a scanty living—usually for no more than two months in the year—as they can where groundwater appears in sufficient quantities to supply cisterns. In addition, there are oases—fertile, well-watered "islands"—where farmers can tend date palms, vegetables, and other crops.[1]

THE RISE OF ISLAM

According to moviemakers' stereotypes, nomads wander the desert like gypsies; they live a life of idleness in their tents and occasionally rob travelers or plunder the villages of hard-working peasants. In fact the nomad's life requires great skill, specialized aptitudes, and a high degree of managerial competence. Since antiquity nomads have had to keep on the move, following the rainy season, their lives revolving around the needs of their herds and the vagaries of the weather. This migratory rhythm varies in accordance with local particularities and the kinds of animals that the nomads tend—donkeys, sheep, camels. But essentially nomadic peoples, whether ancient Hebrews or modern Arab bedouins, Tuareg or Somali, require similar skills; the logistics of their existence are determined by water and pastures, so that accurate "staff work" is a matter of life or death. Movement is affected by many factors: the nature of the rainfall, the prevalence of disease, the availability of salt for stock, and the competition, according to lineage, for access to the same pastures and water holes. The seasons are by no means constant, for annual rainfall varies considerably. The nomad must take advantage of a chance shower or downpour; since animals quickly denude grazing lands, he must move quickly. Both men and beasts rapidly exhaust the water available in wells and cisterns.

The animals best adjusted to life in the desert are goats, sheep, donkeys, and camels. Of these only the camel can move over long distances. Its introduction (about 800 B.C. or possibly earlier) revolutionized life in the desert. The camel not only supplied its owners with milk and wool; it allowed them extraordinary mobility. Nomadic leaders organized treks over long distances, an ability easily applied to planning military compaigns. The bedouins were able to cross great deserts on camel-back where no conventional armies could follow. Not surprisingly, nomadic life bred natural warriors, inured to hardship. A pastoral existence, since it depended on the cohesion of the clan, provided bands with a strong sense of discipline and loyalty. Life in arid lands also engendered quarrels between clans competing for access to scarce water and good pastures, so the virtues of the warrior were prized. Able to sustain great privation, trained from childhood in the use of arms, proud, dedicated to the cult of avenging slights or injuries inflicted on the community, pastoral peoples easily became magnificent irregular cavalry that was able to move at great speed, and was always ready to retreat into the forlorn wasteland where foot soldiers or even horse-driven chariots could not easily follow.[2]

The men of the desert grew to be specialists, dependent on their neighbors for goods of all sorts. Since the dawn of history nomads have exchanged goods with the dwellers of more fertile lands, bartering animals for grain and other commodities. Desert skills could be applied easily to long-distance trade, especially when camels came into wide use. Merchants developed elaborate techniques for organizing the exchange of such commodities as salt, gold, ivory, and spices. All this merchandise weighed little but cost a great deal: it was therefore capable of bearing the considerable expense involved in long-distance caravan traffic.

The organization of caravans became a highly specialized trade as complex as the shipping business. The great Middle Eastern cities of antiquity knew an extensive traffic in silk, spices, jewelry, and other luxury products, and in such necessities as dates, skins, hides, and grain. By the early medieval period cities like Baghdad, Cairo, and Damascus were far more splendid than any urban center in Europe. It is hard to generalize about their physical layout and social structure. Suffice it to say that they all depended in varying measure on commerce, on administration, and on their craftsmen—weavers, dyers, tailors, silversmiths, carpetmakers, and many others. Major cities were usually defended by walls and divided into separate quarters. The government section often contained the ruler's palace, the army barracks, and a place of worship. Even more important was the bazaar, a noisy, crowded, smelly, picturesque labyrinth of crooked alleyways, often covered, that served the needs of traders and travelers. The cities were connected by ties of political allegiance to a lord or king whose armies and civil service they helped to sustain. Even more important as a social cement was the great migrant population of itinerant hawkers, preachers, holy men, tax gatherers, storytellers, jugglers, soothsayers, and traders who kept the urban centers in touch with one another and with the most remote oases and mountain hamlets of the hinterland.

The majority of Middle Easterners, then as now, were neither nomads nor townsmen. They were farmers. Villagers supplied food; they paid most of the taxes that sustained the ancient empires. The tiller's way of life was colored by the area in which he lived. A villager in a mountain fastness of the Lebanon had little in common with a peasant working his land in the irrigated plains of Egypt or Mesopotamia. Methods varied from intensive forms of horticulture in the vicinity of cities to rudimentary types of shifting agriculture in the backlands. But all villages shared certain recognizable features. They were commonly organized on a kinship basis. Farmers used fairly simple tools: a light plow, the water wheel, the sickle and scythe. The range of medieval farming in the Middle East was impressive: tillers grew many kinds of cereals, vegetables, lemons, oranges, grapes—products that, by their diversity, astonished medieval travelers from Northern Europe. Villagers supplemented their livelihood by producing clothes, mats, trays, baskets. Such handicrafts made them largely, though not wholly, independent of imported merchandise.

Middle Eastern society thus comprised within itself four distinct though complementary forms of society: the society of mountaineers, the nomad band, the city, and the farming community. Politically the region was overshadowed by great empires whose power grew and contracted in accordance with the vicissitudes of religion, trade, kinship, and war. During the seventh century A.D., the era in which Islam rose to power, the two most powerful states in the Middle East were the Byzantine Empire, heir to Rome in the eastern Mediterranean and dominating what are now Syria, Palestine, Egypt, Greece, and Turkey; and its rival the Sassanid Empire, the second superpower of the Middle East, governing what are now Iran and Iraq.

The Arab Peninsula formed part of the hinterland, a rural periphery that was more backward but was linked by many ties to the great cities of the river plains and the Mediterranean littoral. The desert tribes were still pagan, governed by elected leaders drawn from powerful lineages. But here and there settled nomads established small or medium-sized towns, as well as cities like Mecca, that submitted to an oligarchy of merchant families. Persian, Byzantine, and Syrian cultures permeated the Arab periphery through trade, foreign settlements in the interior, and occasional attempts at conquest. The men of the desert thus grew familiar with foreign cultures—the religions of Jews, Christians, and Zoroastrians—and with literacy, new forms of economic organization, and new ways of waging war.

Mohammed

Such was the world of Mohammed (Muhammad), the most outstanding leader in the history of the Middle East and, according to his followers, the greatest personality in world history. Mohammed was born in Mecca sometime between 570 and 580 A.D., the son of a respectable merchant family. He acquired some wealth by marrying the widow of a trader, and himself gained experience in commerce. On approaching middle age he received what he considered a divine call to preach God's message. His early supporters came mainly from the ranks of the poor, and he was forced to flee his native city for Medina. Muslims date history from this flight, the *hegira* or *hijra* of 622 A.D. Mohammed became a successful ruler who established peace between the warring factions of his adopted city. He also proved his mettle as a successful military leader and subsequently established his dominion over many communities, including Mecca.

But Mohammed was infinitely more than a successful warrior and statesman. When he died in 632 A.D. he had carried through a religious and social revolution; he had established a new community of faith in which religious affiliation supplemented—and in some sense transcended—kinship. His was a theocratic government that in its own estimation derived its legitimacy from God.

Mohammed's inspiration found expression in the Qur'an (Koran), the world's most influential text next to the Bible. Muslims regard the Qur'an as God's revelation to Mohammed. Except for the first verse and a few passages attributed to Mohammed or the angels, the speaker throughout is God himself. Islam is an intensely God-centered religion; the very name Islam means "submission" to the will of God. The Qur'an begins with a prayer worthy in its dignity to rank with the Psalms:

> In the name of God, the Compassionate, the Merciful.
> Praise be to God, Lord of the worlds!
> The Compassionate, the Merciful!
> King on the day of reckoning!
> Thee only do we worship and to Thee do we cry for help.
> Guide us on the straight path,
> The path of those to whom Thou has been gracious,
> With whom Thou art not angry, and who go not astray.

In formulating his creed Mohammed wove Jewish and Christian strands into a new system of thought, simple in design yet colorful and impressive, like a carpet designed by a nomad artist. The Muslim's Confession of Faith—unlike the Christian's Creed—is brief, capable of being memorized by the most backward shepherd boy within a few minutes:

> There is no God but God;
> Mohammed is the Apostle of God.

Islam emphasizes the unity of God, as against the Christian Trinity. God's divine nature is expounded through an enumeration of his various qualities under the three categories of power, unity, and goodness. God's throne is surrounded by angels who praise their Divine King and who serve as his messengers. God created the world in six days and set Adam in paradise. But tempted by Satan, a fallen angel, Adam fell. God revealed himself to the sons of Adam through prophets, to some of whom he gave a book: Moses received the Torah, Jesus the Gospel, Mohammed the Qur'an. Mohammed is the last of the prophets; none shall follow in his ministry.

The religious duties incumbent on the believer are simple. The Muslim must recite the creed at least once a day with a full understanding of its meaning and a sincere conviction of its truth. Every Muslim is required to worship God five times a day; he is obliged to fast during the month of Ramadan; he must give alms to the needy according to a prescribed code. And once in his lifetime a Muslim should, if he is able to do so, perform the pilgrimage to Mecca.[3]

The Islamic Way

The religious impact of Islam was staggering. For a time no competing creed seemed capable of prevailing against Mohammed's message. Mohammed's straightforward monotheism—both grandiose and austere—was infinitely superior in the intellectual and moral sense to the pagan creeds supplanted by Islam. The new faith, contrasting divine perfection with human inadequacy, profoundly shaped the believers' life. To this day, to give but small examples, a Muslim carpet weaver will deliberately introduce a small flaw into the pattern of his handiwork, thereby showing that perfection belongs alone to God; or a small boy may be harshly reprimanded by his teacher in an Islamic school for asserting that rain is bound to fall tomorrow, because such confidence is a form of hubris that does not befit a human creature. More importantly, Islam claimed to comprehend within itself the other two monotheistic creeds of mankind, Judaism and Christianity, and even to transcend them. Islam's spiritual conquests thereby came to parallel its earthly victories.

In struggling for religious supremacy against its various rivals in the Middle East, Islam enjoyed a number of distinct advantages. Judaism, in its later Rabbinical form, was a creed readily practiced by traders and craftsmen; history even records the conversion of some nomadic tribes such as the Khazars. But Rabbinical Judaism had little appeal to peasants of a traditional kind. Perhaps a fairly substantial number of medieval Jews in Europe and the Middle East made their living as wine growers, gardeners, or truck farmers—agricultural pursuits linked to a market economy. But postexilic Judaism almost never became a peasant's creed. A traditional cultivator in the Atlas Mountains, in the valley of the Rhone, or in the valley of the Rhine could not easily practice a creed that minutely regulated every aspect of living, including land management, according to the dictates of life as it had been lived in ancient Palestine. Christianity was more flexible. Its practice could adjust to the needs of peasants and townsmen alike. But ecclesiastical Christianity held no appeal for nomadic peoples, who could not afford the heavy capital investment required in the building of churches or in the maintenance of an elaborate ecclesiastical hierarchy and professional priesthood.

Islam, alone among the three great religions, appealed equally to farmer, nomad, and townsman, the three pillars of Middle Eastern society. Backward villagers understood the simplicities of a religion that was in tune with their lives. Islam was even more successful among nomads. The life of an Arab or a Somali or a Tuareg herdsman allowed much time for contemplation. Extended periods of leisure; the solitude, the immensity, and the perils of the desert; the constant proximity of death; all easily induced the bedouins and other nomads of his kind to wonder about the meaning of life, the existence of God, his mercy, his splendor, his limitless power. As a modern traveler has put it, "to these Bedu, God is a reality, and the conviction of his presence gives them the courage to endure. For them to doubt his existence would be as inconceivable as to blaspheme."[4]

But Islam was not simply the religion of the countryside and the desert. Mohammed was a townsman familiar with the life of the city. In legislating for the city of Medina, he bore in mind the needs of small traders and craftsmen and praised hard work, enjoining the faithful to save for themselves and to respect the property of others. Mohammed also considered the needs of the poor. He prohibited the practice of usury, which he regarded as an illegitimate form of hoarding; he insisted on almsgiving to help the needy. His creed formed a new bond of union that linked cultivators, townsmen, and nomads into a community of faith—a community that all could enter.

Muslims looked upon unbelievers with disdain. They abhorred idolatry. Jews and Christians they regarded as inferior to themselves. But unlike the Christians, who in medieval times considered Mohammed an imposter led astray by the devil (or even as a resentful and renegade cardinal balked of election to the papacy) Muslims accorded both Moses and Jesus an honorable place in their theology. Jews and Christians, "people of the Book," received a limited measure of toleration under Islamic governance, a status that compared favorably with that allotted to Jews by most medieval Christian communities. Islam suffered from bitter internal dissension but from nothing comparable in ferocity to the Christian wars of religion that devastated, say, thirteenth-century Provence or seventeenth-century Germany.

Critics have often represented Islam as an inflexible creed founded on an unchanging law that cannot readily meet altering social circumstances. Islam in actual fact, though recognizing no formal distinction between politics and theology, between the secular and the religious spheres of life, was capable of considerable adjustment in the light of changing conditions. The Sunnis, or Sunnites, the most numerous and ancient Muslim group, derived their name from the *sunna* or "path," that is, the customary practice of Mohammed as set forth in the Hadith (traditions). The Muslim theologians of the medieval period developed an elaborate science of criticism to distinguish those Hadiths thought genuine from those that seemed spurious. To the Qur'an and the Hadith, the Sunnis, beginning in medieval times, added *ijmā*, the universal consent held to justify beliefs not formally warranted by the Qur'an or by tradition. The fourth foundation stone of Islam, according to the Sunnis, was *qiyās* (analogy), a mode of argument by which a belief or practice is justified on the grounds that it is similar though not identical to a tenet embodied in the Qur'an, in tradition, or in consent.

Thus armed, Muslim thinkers created an elaborate theology based on the predestination of good and evil and on a complex system of law and philosophy enriched by ancient Greek, Jewish, and even Christian speculations. Islam resembled Judaism more than it did Christianity. But where the Jews looked to the future, to the arrival of the Messiah, Islam was directed to the present. Muslim eschatology predicted an end of time, as did Jewish and Christian eschatology. Yet Islam was more oriented to the present than either. Mohammed had put the final "seal" upon prophecy; all the problems of faith had apparently been solved.

The Golden Age of Islam

According to the Bible, Abel, the shepherd, and Cain, the tiller of the soil, were brothers born to Adam and Eve. Herdsmen and cultivators in the Middle East had subsisted in a close though uneasy partnership from time immemorial. But peaceful trade and traffic were continuously interrupted by war. The nomads raided their settled neighbors, especially in times of drought and scarcity, and the agriculturists pushed into the pastoralists' well-watered grazing grounds. The Book of Genesis recounts that the original aggressor was Cain, the farmer, who slew Abel because "the Lord had respect unto Abel and his offering. But unto Cain and his offering he had no respect."[5]

In their wars against the cultivators, the herdsmen had many advantages— mobility, hardihood, and fighting skill. When the men of the desert could overcome the perpetual quarrels between hostile clans, the nomads were formidable foes. The great Arab advance may have been due in part to the demographic pressure that built up in the arid lands of the Arab Peninsula and to the fact that preceding conflicts between Byzantium and Persia had left both superpowers exhausted. Islam and the new forms of political organization set up under Islamic auspices provided the tools of conquest. The nomads had a new creed and a new political cohesion that for a time rendered them irresistible. To quote Bernard Lewis, Arab strategy was determined by the use of desert power on lines strikingly similar to the use of modern seapower. The nomads knew the desert; their enemies did not. The Arabs used the desert as a means of communication and supply, and as a retreat in time of need. In each of the conquered provinces the Arabs established their main bases in towns on the edge of the desert and sown land. These garrison towns became the strongholds of the early Arab Empire, holding its garrisons and the main centers of government.[6]

Arab power spread with startling rapidity. In 636 A.D. the Arabs inflicted a crushing defeat on the Byzantine Empire, placing the whole of Syria and Palestine at the mercy of Islam. Within a century they held sway from the Pyrenees on the border of France to the Pamirs in Central Asia. Lands formerly subject to the Persian monarchy—Arabia, Syria, Palestine, all Byzantine territory south of the Taurus Mountains, the whole of North Africa and distant Spain—were welded into an empire that stretched across three thousand miles. For a time it overshadowed the conquests of Alexander the Great and Julius Caesar. This enormous empire was held together by the Islamic religion, by the use of Arabic as a common linguistic bond, by a policy of limited toleration guaranteeing freedom of religion to Jews and Christians, and by a missionary policy that permanently removed North Africa, Syria, Palestine, and ultimately Anatolia—once the heartlands of Christianity—from the Christian world. The Muslims, Arab and non-Arab alike, created a new civilization that melted the cultural legacies of the Arabs, the Greeks, the Jews, the Persians, and many other peoples into a new amalgam.

Commerce and civilization The new Arabo-Islamic civilization was a great complex of interlocking trading systems. The prophet Mohammed had earned his living in commerce as a representative of Mecca, a city engaged in caravan trade over all Arabia. Islam thus honored the trader; there were no restrictions on trafficking with Christians, Jews, or unbelievers. Islamic merchants linked the Mediterranean Basin to the Red Sea, the Persian Gulf, and the Indian Ocean. Muslim fleets for a time dominated the Mediterranean. Arab traders sailed their *dhows* all the way to East Africa, Madagascar, Ceylon, and India. By the end of the eighth century Arab vessels had reached distant China. In addition, Arab, Jewish, and Byzantine merchants made good use of riverine communications; they established a trading route from the Caspian Sea along the Volga River to the barbarian lands of the Baltic. Sea and river routes intersected with overland routes used by camel caravans that stretched across the Sahara and the Arabian Desert, and extended all the way to China. From the late seventh to the end of the twelfth centuries the Arab Empire acted much like a giant free-trade area, more vast than any other in previous history.[7]

This far-flung traffic primarily involved such luxury goods as animal skins, spices, pedigreed animals, arms, pearls, rare fruit, silk, carpets, and high-quality weapons. It therefore mainly served the needs of the rich and wellborn. The system, however, interlocked with even more extensive networks of local commerce in which craftsmen, farmers, nomads, and fishermen exchanged the necessities of life.

Muslim commerce had far-reaching consequences. Men and merchandise moved over an enormous area; living standards rose, certainly for the ruling classes and to a lesser extent for their subjects. The new civilization was impressive in its technology. Persian, Arab, Jewish, Greek, Copt, and Armenian intellectuals excelled in many sciences—botany, pharmacy, medicine, mathematics, cartography, astronomy, chemistry—and in the arts of trade, navigation, and other branches of practical knowledge. To this day the Arab legacy in Europe remains embodied in such words of Arabic derivation as "traffic," "tariff," "chemistry" (from al-kīmīya', "alchemy") "algebra," "admiral," and "zenith." Muslim craftsmen, as did their Christian and Jewish colleagues, produced a great variety of tools and scientific instruments and a broad range of articles of common use. Muslim agronomists were pioneers in scientific farming. Muslim engineers excelled in the construction of water mills, used for grinding grain and for industrial purposes, of water clocks, and of complex devices for raising the water level—devices essential to irrigation and urban water supply.

Arab trade, like Arab innovations in science, literature, philosophy, art, architecture, and technology, spread far afield, reaching early medieval Europe through Islamic Spain, Italy (especially Sicily), and Byzantium. Muslim civilization spread across the Sahara into the great Sudanic belt of Africa, into East Africa, India, Indonesia, and far into Central Asia. Arabic became the principal language of religion, literature, and scholarship.

"There is no victor but God"   Equally impressive was the Arab achievement in architecture and the decorative arts. Early Arab architecture was even more austere than the stark Romanesque styles of medieval Europe. The Great Mosque at Kairouan in North Africa, for instance, built and enlarged during the seventh and eighth centuries A.D., to this day impresses the visitor by its severity. The walls are blank; the courtyard, massive in its simplicity, leads to a huge hypostyle hall punctuated on its axis by two cupolas. The minaret from which the muezzin calls the faithful to prayer is massive and square, decorated with a few simple arches. The Islamic religion has no need for a professional priesthood in the Catholic sense; believers need no intermediary to intercede for them with God; all are equal within the large central space. The arts, when not eschewing the representation of images for religious reasons, carry the same emphasis on geometrical form and give much less scope to the picturing of living beings, whether men or beasts, than do most other artistic traditions.

With the growing complexity of Muslim society and the spread of wealth and luxury, artistic forms grew more intricate. The open space within the mosque now became a court; the higher central nave provided an axis to the composition of the mosque. The number of doors diminished, so that the building lost some of its immediate accessibility to the people. High minarets rose into the sky, towers to call the faithful to prayer and to dominate the Muslim city by their solidity. Wall surfaces, once bare, were covered by elaborate mosaics or stucco work to give a new visual dimension to their planes, and emphasis was given to the use of sunlight and shade. The famous Alhambra in Spain, completed in the thirteenth century, is infinitely subtle in its changing forms—

open and covered space combine and contrast with light and darkness. Oleg Grabar, an art historian, describes columns that are brilliantly lit at night only to recede during the day to become dark frames around the sunlight. One interpretation likens the Court of the Lions to an earthly representation of paradise. Another version calls the Alhambra an embodiment in stone of the Muslim tenet, affirmed over and over again in inscriptions that grace the building, that nothing seen or fashioned by men is real since "there is no victor but God."[8]

At the same time there was a striking change in the art of the great Muslim princes, art which had always drawn on foreign inspiration, especially that of the Copts, Byzantines, Armenians, and Persians. Princely art traditionally employed lifelike representations in woodwork, ivory carving, and wall paintings. The height of this splendor and of artistic realism was reached in the twelfth and thirteenth centuries, when art works of all kinds suddenly became animated with images. There was a fascination with lifelike representation, with the marvels of this world. Ceramics, glassware, metal work, and mosaics displayed pictures illustrating almost every subject of interest to man. Books were embellished with miniatures that displayed a wealth of practical observation.

The new styles expressed the excitement, the joie de vivre, and the vitality of an era when Islamic civilization was at the height of its achievement. Muslim philosophy and literature were unequaled in their perceptivity; from Anatolia to India, Islam made new conquests; a new Hispano-Arabic civilization had grown to maturity. The Crusaders from the West were finally repelled. Acre, the last Christian stronghold in the Holy Land, fell in 1291 after a long era of conflict that had begun in 1095 with the First Crusade. It was then that Arab philosophy profoundly influenced Western thought. Arab scholarship played a major part in refreshing Christian familiarity with the legacy of ancient Greece; Arab philosophers like Averroës (Arabic name of ibn-Rushd, 1126–1198 A.D.) became household words to Western academics.

THE DECLINE OF ARAB CIVILIZATION

The sudden decline in the quality of Arab civilization began in the middle of the fourteenth century. Arab letters continued to produce some outstanding writers, but the classical inspiration was rarely recaptured. Arab savants continued their research, but gradually yielded their leadership in the exact sciences and in classical scholarship to their colleagues in the West. In the representational arts, the Arab fascination with lifelike imagery waned.

The causes of this decline are hard to trace. They have nothing to do with the Arab people as such, for Arab civilization—the point bears repeating—

was a complex mosaic incorporating the work of Spaniards and Persians, Jews and Syrians, Byzantines and Indians, Armenians and Africans. Not surprisingly, al-Ma'arru (973–1057 A.D.), one of the greatest poets in Arab letters, had celebrated the unity of mankind:

> To humankind, O brother, consecrate
> Thy heart, and shun the hundred Sects that prate
> About the things they little know—about—
> Let all receive thy pity, none thy hate
> . . . .
> For my religion's love, and love alone.[9]

The Arabo-Islamic world, however, could not maintain its political unity. Neither the lavish extravagance of great courts nor the rising expenditure on immense bureaucracies and standing armies were matched by new technological advances. The Arabs had to contend with new barbarian invaders from the east—Turks, and then the Mongols—whose conquests led to the breakdown of civil government in Iraq and the collapse of the irrigation works on which its prosperity depended. A later Mongol force under Timur (Tamerlane) ravaged Syria. Plagues, locusts, and the ravages of bedouin tribes completed the work of the Mongol invaders and further weakened the Islamic world.

The greatest disasters came from the West. In 1498 a Portuguese vessel commanded by Vasco da Gama rounded the Cape of Good Hope and dropped anchor at Calicut. When some astonished Tunisian traders asked what the devil had brought the Franks thus far, the Portuguese navigator allegedly replied, "Christians and spices." They had come to save souls for Catholicism, to purchase pepper, to find friends—and to wage war against Islam.

The Portuguese lacked numbers and were operating at a great distance from their metropolitan base. But their technical equipment, fighting prowess, navigational skill, and morale were unsurpassed. The Muslims had no vessels capable of fighting successfully against Portuguese ships built to withstand Atlantic gales, and the Portuguese mastered the Indian Ocean with astonishing ease. They penetrated to the Persian Gulf and the Red Sea. They preyed on Arab shipping. In a wider sense, the Muslim Near East was outflanked and command of the ocean rapidly passed to the Christians. Muslim fleets permanently lost control of the Indian Ocean. Worse still, perhaps, no Muslim navigator or fighting man took part in the conquest of the New World.

Scholars still dispute the reasons for the decline of the Muslim world and its glories. Some emphasize such internal divisions among the Arabs as the struggles between the orthodox Sunnis and the heterodox Shi'ite sect, which derived its strength from the discontented Mawali (Muslims who were not full members by descent from an Arab tribe). Other interpretations stress economic factors: the Islamic Near East, it is argued, was gradually transformed from a commercial to an essentially feudal economy based in the main on subsistence agriculture and only secondarily on trade.

Ibn Khaldoun (1332–1406), perhaps the greatest Arab philosopher and historian of record, found the essence of Arab history in the never-ending struggle between the "town" and the "desert." The men of the desert, according to Ibn Khaldoun, have glaring faults; they are the enemies of civilization and of all people are the least fit to rule. Nevertheless, these nomads have their virtues. They are tough, disciplined, self-reliant. Above all, they have a peculiar quality essential to the existence of commonwealths: *'asabiyya,* that public spirit or social solidarity, a special virture that transcends the ties of clientage and kinship. Moses had taught *'asabiyya* to the children of Israel when they were wandering in the desert for forty years, thus enabling them to change from a nation of slaves to a nation of conquerors. Mohammed had conjured up the spirit of *'asabiyya* among Arab nomads, who thereby became conquerors and created kingdoms. Kingdoms, however, flourish only so long as *'asabiyya* and the sophistication of the conquered cities remain in balance. In the end, urban sophistication prevails. The nomadic conquerors are corrupted by luxury and vice. The splendid courtiers become parasites; the tax gatherers turn into locusts hated by the people; decadence sets in—until the next invasion of nomadic conquerors repeats the cycle.[10]

THE OTTOMAN ACHIEVEMENT

Whatever the reasons, most Arabic-speaking peoples of the cities and the plains lost their independence. Arabic-speaking villagers and nomads in remote mountain areas and in the desert managed their lives largely without outside interference. But the cultivated plains of Iraq, Syria, and Egypt came under foreign rule. The Ottomans, originally a nomadic people from Central Asia, converted to Mohammed's creed and created a powerful military monarchy. In 1453 they captured Constantinople, which had become the new Rome. The works of art that had adorned this Western city disappeared and it changed in character; the population became oriental in dress and appearance. The greatest of Christian churches, Hagia Sophia, was converted to a mosque. The new sultans constructed a splendid seraglio and great mosques that incorporated both Byzantine and eastern features.

The Ottomans adapted many Byzantine institutions to their own purposes and the Ottoman monarchy in certain respects revived and continued the splendors of Byzantium. Constantinople became the center of what was—for a time—the world's greatest military power. Ottoman administration was—for a time—efficient. Turkish armies, superbly equipped with artillery, were more formidable than any raised in Europe. Ottoman navies dominated the greater part of the Mediterranean. Their first major defeat was the Christian naval victory at Lepanto in 1571, but this far from destroyed Turkish strength.

The Ottoman achievement was magnificent. Ottoman suzerainty spread over the whole of North Africa as far as the frontiers of Morocco. Egypt and Syria, now the main centers of Arab culture, were firmly under Ottoman control. The Ottomans established a powerful empire in southeastern Europe. In 1629 and again in 1683 Ottoman armies stood at the gates of Vienna. Had the Ottomans taken the imperial city, Austria—incredible as it now sounds—might have become a partly Islamicized country and they might have penetrated even further into Central Europe, divided as it was by bitter social conflict and by wars between Protestants and Catholics.

Ottoman rule was often popular. The Ottomans frequently governed with a lighter hand than had the Christian feudal magnates whom they displaced. (Popular plays in sixteenth-century Germany showed a victorious sultan welcomed as their saviour by downtrodden peasants.) Islamic rule seemed to offer other advantages. Ottoman rulers, like their Arab predecessors, were relatively tolerant of non-Muslim religions. The seventeenth-century tag *cujus regio ejus religio* (freely, "the ruler dictates his subjects' faith") was not a Muslim precept; it was Christian. This toleration had its advantages for the Ottoman monarchy. Many Jews expelled from Spain in 1492 took refuge in Ottoman dominions—to the astonishment of the Turkish monarch, as the story goes, who commented that the Castilian king in his folly impoverished himself to enrich his rival.

The Ottomans developed a literature of their own that rivaled that of the Persians. Both Turkish and Persian letters, essentially independent of Arabic, were under Arabic influence. Arabic as a language had not lost all inspiration. Arab intellectuals continued to write poetry, romances, theological and historical works, travelogues, and even scientific or philosophical treatises. But some of its universal quality was gone. Except for a limited number of theological and philosophical studies, the literary use of Arabic was confined to Arabic-speaking countries. Islamic civilization, however, reached new heights in Persia, where the sixteenth century witnessed a new magnificence in architecture and painting, and also in India. The Ottomans had superb achievements to their credit in letters as well as in war. The classic period of Turkish literature began in the sixteenth century with writers like Fuzuli and Baki.

Sixteenth-century Europeans looked upon Islamic achievement with a mixture of fascination and fear. What did the discoveries in the New World matter when the Turks had advanced into the heart of Europe? The Ottoman monarchy was formidable by reason of its military strength and its skill in exploiting every social discontent among the conquered. Even the imperial ambassador at Constantinople, as the historian H. R. Trevor Roper records, had to respect the Ottomans' civic virtue, their military prowess, their frugality, the impressive nature of their public works, their charitable enterprise, and the relative facility with which men of lowly social origin could rise to the highest posts in the land.[11] Had a space traveler suddenly descended on sixteenth-century Europe he might well have concluded, after consulting the experts of the time, that Islam was bound to prevail over a divided and war-torn West.

The Turk in Retreat

But the Muslim world did not prevail over the West. The tide of battle turned and Ottoman power began to recede in Europe. The treaty of Karlowitz (Karlovici), signed in 1699 between Austria, Poland, Venice, and Turkey, forced the sultan to yield many Ottoman conquests. The Austrians continued to advance at Turkey's expense and so did the Russians. The peace treaty of Küçuk Kainarca (Kuchuk Kainardji) in 1774 was the most humiliating document that the Turks had ever signed; not only did the sultan have to make major territorial concessions but he was forced to give Russia the right to protect the Sultan's Greek Orthodox subjects. Turkey had ceased to be a great power; its decay was manifest, its future dubious. The "Eastern question" of the future no longer dealt with the defense of Christendom but with the problem of how best to despoil the sultan of his dominions without causing wars among his despoilers.

It is not easy to disentangle the reasons for the decay of the Turkish Empire. The Turkish army in its heyday consisted of regular soldiers recruited from the captured sons of Christians, sworn to celibacy, and trained to form a privileged military elite. The "janissaries" (infantry) and "spahis" (cavalry) were supported by a strong reserve force drawn mainly from the feudal retinue of Muslim nobility; more than half of it was recruited in Europe. The trained armies were supported by irregular mountaineers from the Balkans and Anatolia. The greatest part of the Turkish army, in other words, came from southeastern Europe, not from the Orient. During the eighteenth and nineteenth centuries, however, discipline in the professional forces declined; their privileges became a source of political danger and the nobility grew increasingly independent of the sultan's authority. The quality of the military personnel saw a similar regression.

According to Bernard Lewis, the halting of the Ottoman advance in Europe was comparable in some ways to the closing of the frontier in the United States, but its effects were far more shattering.[12] The Ottoman state had been born on the frontier between Islam and Byzantine Christianity; it was organized for war and thus provided work and rewards for soldiers, administrators, and men of religion. The Ottoman system of government, taxation, and land tenure were geared to the needs of an expanding society. Once the frontier began to recede, Ottoman institutions could no longer cope with the country's needs.

Military and political decline accompanied economic decay. The Turks could not compete with Westerners on the high seas. The Ottomans had no share in the trade of the New World and they were driven from the Indian Ocean. The influx of precious metals from Latin America, a consequence of Western colonization in the New World, struck the Ottoman monarchy with devastating severity. Ottoman currency was eroded by inflation; measures taken by the government further debased the coinage. Faced with a growing expenditure and a depreciating currency, the demands of the Ottoman treasury grew more exacting. The bureaucracy, oversized and underpaid, became increasingly corrupt. The shrinking economy of the empire had to support a splendid court, a huge administrative machine, a religious hierarchy, and a parasitic class of tax farmers and absentee landlords. Yet the technological level of agriculture remained low; there were no agronomical or industrial advances equal to those achieved from the sixteenth and seventeenth centuries onward in northwestern Europe. The Islamic nations fell behind in science and scholarship as well as in engineering, logistics, and military pursuits.

Turkey's fundamental weakness—one shared with all Islamic states in India, Persia, or North Africa—went deeper. All these states lacked an active, self-confident, assertive middle class enjoying widespread national support within a unified national culture of the kind found in Western Europe. Countries like Britain, France, or Holland might be riddled by bitter class divisions. But however great the clashes over social issues between noblemen, burghers, peasants, and working men, most of them spoke the same language, shared the same or a similar religion, and adhered to the same cultural norms.

Within much of the Islamic world, as in many parts of Eastern Europe, class and ethnoreligious divisions widely coincided. Ethnoreligious loyalties were further supported by the traditional system of Turkish administration that left the various *millets*, or ethnoreligious communities—Jews, Greeks, Armenians—with extensive powers of internal self-government. The bourgeoisie, divided into scores of ethnoreligious segments, lacked cohesion and were devoid of self-esteem. The merchant princes, shipping owners, and bankers of the Ottoman Empire were as enterprising as any in the West, but they were usually Greeks, Armenians, Jews, Copts—in other words, second-class citizens, unbelievers, subject to social insults and financial exactions on the part of incompetent and corrupt bureaucrats. The middle class could not assert its power, much less lead a revolution. A man's status was largely determined by inheritance. The scope of his economic endeavor was constrained by a backward technology and by backward means of transport; by bureaucratic exactions; by guild regulations and arbitrary imposts that penalized profits; and by habits of religious thought that, far from encouraging individual responsibility, now stressed passivity and surrender of the self to the inscrutable will of God.

The "sick man of Europe"   Throughout the nineteenth century, then, the Ottoman monarchy diminished in power. Persia, Turkey's historic rival in the East, also failed to hold her own. After the murder of Nadir Shah in 1774 Persia went through a period of temporary anarchy that left Russia in the ascendant. The Moghul Empire, a great feudal and Islamic monarchy that had once ruled most of India, likewise decayed. By the end of the eighteenth century Great Britain had become the strongest power by far in India and destined to rule over it.

Splendid as these empires had been in their time, they all failed to create political constitutions or a sense of national cohesion in the Western sense. The powers that the Prophet Mohammed and his immediate successors had held in their own persons as rulers, military commanders, judges, and legislators were never formally separated. Many of the great Muslim dynasties succeeded in creating a binding law of succession. Of contenders for the succession there were many in polygamous societies where princes had a far more numerous progeny than their Christian counterparts; all too often the pretenders settled the issue through dagger and poison. Western words such as "nation," "democracy," "self-government," or the "rights of man" had no more application in the world of late eighteenth-century Islam than had the spirit of scientific experimentation, sociological inquiry, or modern historical research. The Ottomans had a highly structured bureaucracy with elaborate surveys of property boundaries and complex tax records. From the eighteenth century onward some enlightened Turkish travelers pondered deeply on the misfortunes of their country and on the secret of Western success. Yet a nineteenth-century Turkish governor could still answer an English scholar's request for demographic, economic, and historical information by these lines:

MY ILLUSTRIOUS FRIEND AND JOY OF MY LIVER!

The thing you ask of me is both difficult and useless. Although I have passed all my days in this place, I have neither counted the houses nor have I inquired into the number of the inhabitants; and as to what one person loads on his mules and the other stows away in the bottom of his ship, that is no business of mine. But, above all, as to the previous history of this city, God only knows the amount of dirt and confusion that the infidels may have eaten before the coming of the sword of Islam. It were unprofitable for us to inquire into it. O my soul! O my lamb! Seek not after the things which concern thee not. Thou camest unto us and we welcomed thee: go in peace.[13]

No modern state, however, could function without the kind of data that the Turkish dignitary so courteously declined to furnish, and in the long run no traditional Islamic polity could resist a modern Western state.

The Western assault on the Islamic world was military, industrial, and political. Cultural exchange was of course a two-way process; European romantic writers, for example, owed a profound debt to Arab literature. (Goethe, Germany's greatest poet, thus derived inspiration from the artistry of the Mu'allaquat, a monument of early Arab poetry.) But the Muslims had to contend with new and dangerous ideas. French revolutionary notions slowly began to filter into the Ottoman Empire by the end of the eighteenth century, first captivating the minds of city-bred Christian intellectuals and later of educated Muslims including many *dönme*, descendants of Jewish converts to Islam. It was for nothing that the sultan (in this case Selim III) tried to repudiate the dangerous theories of liberty, equality, and fraternity advocated by the new apostles of the West:

> In this vain belief and preposterous opinion they have erected new principles and set new laws, and established what Satan whispered to them, and destroyed the bases of religions, and made lawful to themselves forbidden things, and permitted themselves whatever their passion desires, and have enticed into their iniquity the common people, who are as raving madmen, and sown sedition among religions, and thrown mischief between kinds and states.[14]

Napoleon's invasion of Egypt (1798) initiated a series of political disasters for Islam. The prestige of Muslim arms was shattered. The Ottoman monarchy was increasingly on the defensive. It had to cope with a new movement of reform: on the Arabian desert frontier of the empire, Muhammad ibn 'Abd al-Wahhab (1703–1787) had proclaimed a puritanical and populist form of Islam that challenged the Ottomans' political legitimacy. More serious still was the threat from the west. Greece, supported by Great Britain and Russia, had by 1830 achieved its independence from Turkey, whose hold on the remaining Turkish possessions in the Balkan Peninsula grew increasingly weak thereafter. Between 1830 and 1848 the French conquered Algeria. The Turks, after a disastrous war against Russia, were forced in 1878 to cede more of their European possessions. Montenegro, Serbia, and Romania all achieved total independence—a new victory for the values of Christian peasant nationalism. The British decisively defeated Egyptian nationalist forces at Tel-el-Kebir in 1882; British influence became supreme in Egypt and, indeed, throughout the eastern Mediterranean. Russia overran the Muslim regions of Central Asia. France, and to a lesser extent Britain, Italy, and Germany, acquired suzerainty over the Muslim parts of Africa.

The development of international trade and banking; the growth of shipping and railways, telegraphs and tramways: printing presses; and the expansion of cash crops further strengthened the Western economic position. Western manufacturers increasingly competed with small-scale craftsmen; teachers and missionaries from the West presented a new challenge to Islamic divines.[15] The first to benefit from Western trading contracts and Western education were apt to be non-Muslims—Jews, Greeks, Christian Arabs from the Lebanon, Armenians, and Copts—with the result that Muslim resentment against these unbelievers tended to grow rather than diminish.

Muslim intellectuals, soldiers, and administrators, impressed by the military superiority of the West, seriously attempted to come to grips with the new challenge. Muhammad Ali (1805–1849), the semi-independent viceroy of Egypt, sought to modernize his country along Western, and especially French, lines. Albanian by birth, Muhammad Ali claimed to be an Ottoman, not an Arab; he surrounded himself with foreigners; his government was in some measure a form of colonization dependent on a (largely Coptic) bureaucracy. He relied on soldiers from Albania and Thrace, on civilian advisers from the Levant, on military and other experts from France. He promoted Western education; he reorganized the country's army and navy on the Western model; he encouraged export crops like cotton for sale to Great Britain; he pacified the Red Sea, where trade revived; he embarked on a policy of territorial expansion into the Sudan, which was a source of slaves, domestic animals, and ivory. Muhammad's projects far exceeded his country's resources and his diplomatic objectives were frustrated by the Great Powers. But he did succeed in weakening the feudal order and in strengthening Egypt's links with the West.

The Ottoman monarchy—the "sick man of Europe," as Czar Nicholas I dubbed it—took a long time to die. The Turks sustained a series of disastrous military defeats. When properly led, however, they could still astonish the world by their tenacity and by their skill in making use of the latest technical innovation. The defense of Plevna (1878), conducted by Osman Pasha against a Russo-Romanian army, was brilliant—though ultimately unsuccessful. During World War I the Turks, supposedly decadent, managed to win a series of victories that experts would have regarded as inconceivable. A British army capitulated at Kut-al-Amara in Mesopotamia in 1915; in the same year the Allies sustained an even greater disaster when the Turks defeated a major British attempt to capture the Dardanelles. But for all the abilities of Turkish intellectuals and Turkish soldiers, the Ottoman monarchy collapsed at the end of World War I.

The reformers had failed to create a sense of Ottoman nationality transcending ethnic nationalism. Neither did they succeed in rallying the Muslims of the empire around the sultan as a defender of the faith. Modern scholarship indicates that Arab nationalism was slow in the making. As late as World War I, most Arabic-speaking Muslims remained loyal to the Ottoman monarchy; their support, however, was mainly passive. There was opposition to the monarchy in remote desert and mountain regions that the sultan could scarcely control. There was also opposition in the cities; much of it was derived from Christian Arabs, who played an important part in the development of Arab nationalism. Whatever moral credit remained to the Ottoman monarchy abroad was dissipated by the savage slaughter of the Armenian minority in 1915. The Ottoman monarchy foundered, together with its German and Austro-Hungarian allies. By 1919 the outlook for Islamic independence was grim. Syria and Lebanon passed under French domination; Great Britain was supreme in Palestine and Iraq. Apart from the crumbling Qajar dynasty in Persia, independent Islamic rule survived in only a few remote areas like Saudi Arabia and Afghanistan. Western ascendancy seemed assured in the lands of the Crescent.

ADAPTATION AND RECOVERY

Turkey was the first Islamic country to recover. At the end of World War I her position seemed desperate. The Treaty of Sèvres, concluded in 1920 between the sultan and the Allies, would have partitioned Turkey between Britain, Greece, Italy, and France, thus largely extinguishing the country's national existence. A Greek army advanced deep into Anatolia, but Turkey rallied and the Greeks were defeated in 1921 and 1922. Turkey was reconstituted as a secular state. The Orthodox Greeks in Anatolia were "exchanged" for the Muslims in Greek-held Macedonia in a brutal displacement of populations that left Turkey ethnically much more homogeneous than ever before. The Ottoman Empire joined the empires of the Habsburgs, Hohenzollerns, and the Romanovs in oblivion.

The End of Western Rule

World War II destroyed the Western European empires as well as obliterating Hitler's so-called Third Reich. The spectacle of yet another bloody conflict in Europe and the sudden collapse of France weakened Western prestige in Asia and Africa. For the first time in their history, the Western colonial powers had to contend with bitter opposition to the very principle of colonialism among a large segment of their own opinion-makers—radio commentators, teachers, clergymen, journalists, and professors. In addition the Western powers were divided among themselves. Thus the British conquest of Libya assured that nation's independence from the Italians, while the British invasion of Vichy-controlled Syria in 1941 precipitated the independence of Syria and Lebanon in 1944.

The decade following the end of World War II saw the demise of British power in the Middle East. Britain, not only weakened by war and economic problems but disillusioned with the splendor of empire, withdrew peacefully from India, Palestine, Egypt, and Iraq. The only failure in this succession of Muslim accomplishments was the loss of Israel, which defeated all Arab counterattacks and achieved her independence in 1948. But the decline of Western European influence in the Middle East continued. In 1956 Great Britain, for the last time, tried to reassert her position by reoccupying the Suez Canal in cooperation with France and Israel. The British only managed to draw upon themselves the anger of the United States and the Soviet Union. They also aroused Arab hostility and, even more important, the bitter opposition of a large segment of the British electorate that opposed the Suez venture on moral and political grounds.

France held on longest in the area. While conceding independence to Morocco and Tunisia in 1956, the French fought a long and agonizing war for Algeria. Though militarily successful, they failed politically. The French could neither inspire their own conscripts with enthusiasm for a long-drawn-out war, nor reconcile the Algerian Muslims to French rule, nor pacify the large section of French public opinion that strongly opposed the Algerian War. In 1962 Algeria became independent. The age of Western European empire in the Middle East had come to an end.

Coming to Terms with the West

Political change brought with it far-reaching social and economic shifts. The traditional structure of Middle Eastern society was shattered beyond repair by oil prospectors, arms salesmen, professors, technicians, journalists, moviemakers, computer experts, industrial entrepreneurs. Land use and life-styles were altered by the spreading use of the internal-combustion engine—the airplane, the truck, the armored car. Communications improved spectacularly, making possible the movement of men and merchandise on a hitherto unimagined scale. As cars and trucks replaced the horse, the donkey, and the camel they eliminated the economic base of nomad life no less efficiently than the plane and the armored car ended the military predominance of irregular mounted cavalry in the wastelands of the interior. The exploitation of Middle Eastern oil resources changed the military and economic balance of power. Instead of waning, Muslim power began to grow, until it affected the world at large.

Faced with such tremendous change, Middle Eastern statesmen and intellectuals were forced to rethink their assumptions. Traditional Muslims had believed that the West could not teach anything to true believers—except, perhaps, a few technological tricks. But Arabs and Turks, obliged from early in the nineteenth century to deal with "Franks" in business, diplomacy, or war, realized that they must come to terms with the West if only in self-defense. In order to meet the Western challenge, and to solve the problems created by weakening religious loyalties and by changes in traditional family relationships, Middle Eastern writers and statesmen evolved a series of new creeds, all of them strongly influenced by the West, often contradictory in their appeal or inclined to overlap with rival ideologies. The intellectual pioneers were Western educated. Lebanese Christians, for example, trained in French or American schools, created the modern Arab press in the latter part of the nineteenth century and their work for a time dominated the Arabic-reading public.

These new creeds showed wide divergence of thought among the Turkish and Arab intellectuals.[16] A small minority was prepared to accept total Westernization. Some of the most ardent advocates of assimilation to the West came from Algeria, a country without a traditional historical identity, since it had been conquered, settled, created, and administered by Europeans more thoroughly than any other Muslim state. French schools produced a new class of Western-educated Algerians; French culture struck root among them. During the first decades of the present century many *évolués* (native Algerians educated in French), though critical of French policy, would willingly have accepted their country's permanent incorporation into France—granted that they received civil and social equality with the *colons* (French colonists) while maintaining their personal status as Muslims. France, however, failed to accord these Gallicized stepsons of hers the same complete acceptance as the Gallicized Germans from Alsace, and the Algerian intellectuals' love for the *métropole* turned into loathing, albeit mixed with respect for the achievements of French civilization.

The most fruitful form of cultural nationalism came from artists who drew inspiration from the West but who used their own vernacular to new purposes. Arabic writers revolted against traditional literary forms and deliberately turned to popular themes and popular speech. The new literary trend began in Egypt and spread to other parts of the Arab world; the result was a renaissance of Arabic literature rivaling comparable movements in Hebrew, Turkish, and Armenian letters. Some Westernizers also drew inspiration from Marxism and came to believe that the true divisions of mankind hinged on social class and not on religious, ethnic, or territorial affinity. Marxism in the Arab world received much of its orignial impetus from members of alien minorities. In Egypt, Marxist pioneers included many Copts and Jews; Algerian communism owed most of its original inspiration to French and other European settlers. Marxist ideology was ill adapted to the needs of countries that did not have a substantial urban proletariat. Most of the Marxist converts came from the ranks of the educated and such theories became popular only when Marxists managed to blend social with religious and national appeals.

The three faces of Arab nationalism   The form of nationalism most familiar to Western Europeans and Americans calls for loyalty to a particular country. Territorial nationalists assume that all inhabitants of a particular nation owe allegiance to the country of their birth or adoption, irrespective of religious and class affinity. Territorial nationalism was strongest in those parts of the Middle East that had relatively clear boundaries, a long tradition of separate political or administrative existence, and a long-settled population—countries like Egypt and Tunisia. In formulating their programs these territorial nationalists considered not merely the Muslim past but also remote antiquity; they exalted the glories of the Pharaohs or of Carthage. Their appeal for loyalty to a common land was real, but they never quite succeeded in transcending ethnoreligious differences. When push came to shove, Iraqi Jews regarded themselves in the first instance as Jews, Maronite Lebanese as Maronites, Turkish Cypriots as Turks. The new Arab states that attained independence after two world wars never gained the kind of undivided loyalty from their citizens that Swedes gave to Sweden or Frenchmen gave to France.

The most popular form of nationalism is ethnolinguistic. It assumes that all men who speak the same tongue form part of one nation and should be members of an independent political unit. Ethnic nationalism is a new invention. Turkish traditionalists regarded the Ottoman Empire as the achievement of the house of Osman fighting for the cause of Islam triumphant; to traditional Ottomans the word "Turk" signified peasant, rustic, or even yokel. But the new ideologists, schooled in the romantic nonsense of European universities, consider the Ottoman monarchy as the achievement of the Turkish or the "Turanian" genius. The ideologues who propound these notions claim to free their nation of Western encroachment. They are in fact enslaved to the European fashions of the day, for the modern usage of "Turk" and "Turanian" derives from European philologists and publicists.[17]

Modern Arab nationalism like modern Zionism is equally syncretic in its origin. The first Zionists, men like Moses Hess and Theodor Herzl, were Westerners more familiar with Goethe than with the Talmud. The pioneers of Arab nationalism were equally Westernized: the founders of the Ba'ath Party in Syria had been educated at the Sorbonne. But they all shared the same enthusiasm for Arab nationhood. While traditional Arabs, like traditional Jews, take pride primarily in their religion, the new ideologues consider Mohammed's message as a providential prelude to the creation of one great Arab nation—as redefined by themselves.

Ethnolinguistic nationalism in the Middle East, however, is never quite free from religious nationalism. Turkish nationalists expect their compatriots to be Sunni Muslims rather than Turkish-speaking Greeks; Zionists normally believe a fully fledged Israeli should be a Jew, not a Lutheran or a Muslim; Iranian nationalists are usually Shi'ites. Arab nationalists are apt to identify their ethnic with their religious identity; they rarely accept Arabic-speaking Jews as Jewish Arabs. According to religious nationalists, nations take their sense of identity from some transcendental creed. Muslims derive their consciousness from Islam; hence Islam must form the cement of the political community. But modern Muslim nationalism is not simply the religion of

Mohammed in a new dress. The Muslim community as conceived by Muslim nationalists or the Jewish community by Zionists is not merely held together by the same faith or by a commitment to live in accordance with a revealed law. According to the tenets of religious nationalism, the Muslim community draws its cohesion from a common inheritance rooted in history. Religion, in other words, serves a multiplicity of purposes, both secular and divine.

For a long time many Westerners were inclined to scoff at Islamic nationalism; indeed, they often continue to consider it a reactionary creed without relevance to the modern world. Lenin or Stalin would have agreed with Lord Cromer, a great Victorian governor, who described Islam as "a body which . . . may yet linger on for centuries, but which is nevertheless politically and socially moribund, and whose gradual decay cannot be arrested by any modern palliatives however skilfully they may be applied."[18]

The Islamic revival   Short-sighted views such as these, later paralleled by Marxist-Leninist prejudices, bear no relation to reality. Islam is a growing and powerful force in the world today. From the Senegal to the Philippines, Muslims are rethinking the fundamentals of their faith. Islam, however, is not a homogeneous movement; Muslims belong to many nations and speak many tongues. The division between the orthodox Sunnis (possibly about 80 percent of the world's Muslims) and the Shi'ites continues; but even among the Sunnis there are many dissenting subgroups. All Muslims share a common set of religious beliefs; all are convinced that Islam should encompass every aspect of life. But the forms taken by the Islamic revival in different parts of the Muslim world vary almost as much as the peoples who profess allegiance to Islam. Islam is not necessarily fanatical, but neither is it necessarily anti-Western. According to Western mythology, the sword of Islam—represented either by fierce Saracens or unspeakable Turks—has been forever raised to strike at the heart of Christendom. Muslims see their history in very different terms. Their civilization, they point out, has been under continuous Western assault since the time of the crusades, as Britons and Frenchmen, Dutch and Italians established great empires that held sway over the bulk of the world's Islamic peoples from Morocco to the East Indies. Political domination goes with economic penetration whose social consequences, according to Muslims, gravely weaken the bonds of religion.

The extreme traditionalists draw inspiration from the works of, among others, Sayyid Abu Al'a Maududi, a Pakistani legal scholar anxious to wean his people from the British imperial legacy. According to their uncompromising Islamic standpoint, sovereignty belongs to God alone; governments are his agents. The Shari'a is the basic law; existing law that conflicts with the Shari'a must be mended or ended. The object of the Islamic state must be to establish the Islamic religion with all its social consequences. (Women, for instance, should be excluded from politics and administration, a policy welcomed by all Muslims who believe in traditional family values, as opposed to the needs of a totally free market economy.) The head of government should be responsible to God alone, a notion that appeals to potentates like Iran's Ayatollah Khomeini, who believes himself to be Allah's Chosen One. The citizens of an Islamic state should form a homogeneous body not subject to divisions such as those of class or ideology. Muslims may not abandon their faith; freedom of religion, oddly enough, is granted only to non-Muslims, who enjoy a limited measure of toleration but should not be eligible for senior posts in the state or even for military service. There can be no equality between men and women, believers and unbelievers, sinners and the righteous. No laws are acceptable that conflict with the Qur'an as interpreted by traditionally minded Muslims. Secularism is equated with atheism, atheism with perdition. In practice, the Islamic state places enormous power into the hands of orthodox Muslim preachers and teachers, who act as guarantors of public purity.

Even the anti-Western Muslim thinkers have assimilated a good deal of Western thought, whether drawn from the traditionalist-romantic legacy of Europe or from its Marxist inheritance. More moderate Islamic reformers have advanced notions comparable in certain respects to those put forward by Catholic social reformers in the nineteenth century. Capitalism, according to their argument, is in its pure form unrestrained by a sense of religious responsibility and therefore leads to the reign of selfishness. Communism, as alien to the spirit of Islam as capitalism, creates an atheist tyranny. Islam, on the other hand, far from being a reactionary and impractical creed, might yet teach mankind to lay the foundations of a new social order. Islam, they believe, provides a Third Way, avoiding the extremes of communism, on the one hand, and free enterprise, on the other. Like capitalism, Islam acknowledges the rights of private property and entitles each citizen to the fruits of his labors. But Islam tempers a free-market economy by emphasizing the citizen's obligation to sustain the poor. The Islamic ideal stresses the right of all to own property; Islamic laws of inheritance, for example, are designed to break up the estate of the deceased among all the heirs, thereby working against the undue concentration of property in a few hands. Islamic finance replaces usury—forbidden by the Qur'an—with new arrangements designed to provide capital on a profit-sharing basis. Such arrangements are embodied in Egypt's Islamic Banks, modeled on the successful cooperative experiment in Mit-Ghamr in that country during the mid-1960s.[19] According to the advocates of Muslim reformism, such models have a wider application and serve as examples for the rest of the world.

In addition, Islam has a revolutionary tradition. Shi'ite Islam, the form practiced by most Iranians, has always emphasized the claims of the poor and powerless struggling against illegitimate authority; yet Shi'ite Islam also contains several factions, some of which have traditionally displayed an apocalyptic tinge. The most extreme of militants, sustained by popular preachers, reject modernity in most of its forms. The more fanatical adherents of Khomeini, for example, loathe America as the Great Satan. They do so, not merely because of what it has or has not done in world politics, but because America to them is a symbol of iniquity. America connotes to them, as Jewry once connoted to the Nazis, all the evil features that supposedly go with the metropolitan life— luxury, corruption, sexual perversion, the destruction of the family, the emancipation of women, pornography . . . the list is endless. This reaction is a worldwide phenomenon; the ayatollah would find many sympathizers in America itself, if he knew how to play his religious cards.

The Islamic militants, however, are disunited. Khomeini stands, not for Islam as a whole, but for a militant form of Shi'ism. For Sunni Muslims, both inside and outside Iran, Khomeini's militance has an alarming quality. Turkish revolutionaries look either to the extreme right or to the extreme left, to ideologies derived from fascism or Marxism rather than to Islam. Khomeini's internal policies have alienated whatever appeal the Islamic revolution may have had for minorities such as the Kurds. Khomeini's old-fashioned puritanism and his unwillingness to grant autonomy to the Turkoman minority of Iran has limited the appeal that the Islamic revolution might have had in Soviet Central Asia. The Iraqi government has suppressed Shi'ite opposition. Khomeini himself looks askance at the revolutionary socialism of Libya, which fuses Islam with a leftist revolution of kinds. Khomeini has no patience with the Wahabi of Saudi Arabia, who look to a pristine form of Islam; he has no answer for the bread-and-butter problems that also concern the Islamic masses in the streets and the bazaars.

No one as yet can foresee the ultimate impact of Islam's resurgence and its ultimate shape. The Islamic revival has taken many different and divisive forms; politically it will be at its most effective as a radical movement among the lower-middle classes and the poor. The Arab masses, unlike the Western educated, have not been much affected by Westernization; the mobs who burned down large stretches of Cairo in 1952 and of Tehran in 1978 sacked the property of aliens—cinemas, department stores, luxury shops—which the poor did not consider to be their own. The Muslim revival once more opens the door to reinterpretation; it is Islam of a revolutionary kind that looks to a better life not merely in the hereafter but also here and now. In certain respects the Muslim revival parallels Zionism. Those Israelis who claim the Holy Land on religious grounds curiously reinforce Muslim revivalists; the adherents of militant Islam now point to the Jews who supposedly have kept their religion for two thousand years and prospered while the Muslims, having abandoned their ancestors' creed, have gone down to defeat. This is heady stuff. Its appeal to the uneducated—Shi'ites as well as Sunnis—remains powerful.

It remains far from clear which of these many Islamic strands—conservative, reformist, or revolutionary—will prevail in the future. But one thing is certain: Islam is not a spent force. Islam remains the most effective social cement to bind the masses. As governments become more popular, they will become more Islamic however leftist their verbiage. The change may bode ill for the non-Muslim communities in the Middle East. As many militants were wont to say during the Egyptian-Israeli War of 1973, "first the Saturday people [the Jews], then the Sunday people [the Christians]." No prophet, however, can predict which course the Islamic resurgence may take. Only one thing is certain: the Crescent is in the ascendant in the Middle East.

The Middle East:
Political, Economic,
and Social Problems

"Middle East" is an arbitrary term invented by the naval historian A. T. Mahan in 1900 to divide the Orient into three sections: the Near East, the Middle East, and the Far East. It reflects the ethnocentric prejudice of Europeans rather than the realities of the Muslim world. In the narrower sense, the Middle East includes Egypt, the lands of the Arabian Peninsula, Turkey, and Iran. In a broader sense, however, the Middle East extends all the way from the Atlantic coast across North Africa through the Fertile Crescent to the eastern border of Iran—and this is the area we are discussing. Some cultural geographers question even this broader definition and consider that territories like Mauritania, Sudan, and Afghanistan should also be included.

Thus defined the area of the Middle East is huge, dwarfing even that of the United States. The distance from Morocco's Atlantic littoral to the Suez Canal is twenty-six hundred miles; a traveler bound from the canal to the Iran-Afghanistan border must traverse another two thousand miles. Geographically, the region includes deserts and alpine mountain lands, Mediterranean coasts reminiscent of southern France, pine forests, and hot, rocky wasteland. There are many subregions, each with its distinctive historical and cultural traditions. There are also non-Arab states such as Turkey, the core of the once-great Ottoman monarchy; Israel, a Jewish state with a large and growing Arab minority; and Iran. Arab states include Egypt, the most populous, and Libya, an oil-rich desert; the states of the Maghreb, Tunisia, Algeria, Morocco, and (by some definitions) Libya, the first three influenced strongly by past French domination; Lebanon, a mixed Muslim-Christian community; Jordan, Syria, Iraq, and the states of the Arabian Peninsula proper—Saudi Arabia, the Yemens,

Kuwait, Bahrein, Oman, the United Arab Emirates, and their neighbors on the Persian Gulf. Outside of Turkey, Israel, and Iran, the principal language is Arabic, but many other tongues are spoken throughout the area: Kurdish, Armenian, Greek, French, and others.

There is no political unity in the Middle East. The numerous sovereign states differ in physical size, armed power, natural resources, and technical sophistication. Many of these states are locked in bitter external disputes: Greece against Turkey, Algeria against Morocco, Libya against Egypt, Iran against Iraq and Afghanistan, Israel against its Arab neighbors. These conflicts are paralleled by internal hostilities between different ethnic groups. Turkey, Iraq, and Iran must deal with discontented Kurdish minorities. Iran parallels the old Austro-Hungarian monarchy in its ethnic diversity and intercommunal disagreements. Lebanon is split between differing Christian and Muslim sects; Israel's population includes many disaffected Arabs. Muslim minorities in Turkey clash with Sunnis; an Alawi Shi'ite minority regime in Syria earns much of its legitimacy from the Sunni majority only by standing as a champion of Islam against Israel. Critics of the existing order take courage variously from an appeal to Arab nationalism, to Muslim fundamentalism, or to different forms of Marxism that share only two features—hatred of the West and of Israel.

The Farmer's Burden

There are, then, many Middle Easts. There is the Middle East of great oil wealth and the Middle East of grinding poverty in the deserts and urban slums; the Middle East of sophisticated trading cities and the Middle East of lonely mountain settlements. Nevertheless, Middle Eastern countries have certain features in common. For all the popular Western stereotypes concerning bedouins and billionaire sheikhs, the majority of Middle Easterners are farmers, many of them poverty-stricken. Pastoral nomadism nowadays employs only a small number of people, and those in remote areas. Farming also provides jobs for men and women engaged in trading crops or in processing them as cotton or tobacco packers, canners, driers, and similar occupations.

Farmers unfortunately must contend with many natural obstacles. The surface of the Middle East is covered by mountains, swamps, semiarid steppes, and shrubland, but most of it is desert. Cultivated areas are small in extent; over the Middle East as a whole they comprise no more than 5.0 to 7.5 percent of the area.[1] The usually high summer temperatures overheat the soils, destroying the organic material within them, and efficient use of fertilizers is difficult. Water is a problem everywhere; more oil is available, in fact, than is clean water. Irrigation is not necessarily the best answer to the productivity problem. Certain soils that seem to be capable of bearing plentiful crops when naturally watered turn saline under irrigation, making economic planning a risky game. In Egypt, for instance, careful use of river dams has turned the lower Nile valley into one of the most productive agricultural regions in the world. The Aswan High Dam project has increased the area of cultivated land in Egypt by one-third, but nearly all the available water in Egypt is now in use—while the population keeps growing. At the same time, water control and heavy irrigation have induced a high degree of salinity in the Nile River delta and have reduced the area's fertility by eliminating the silt formerly brought downriver by floods. Other irrigation schemes—for example, those around Konya in Anatolia and along the Karun River of southwest Iran—have encountered similar difficulties.

These troubles do not exhaust the farmer's woes. The first account of the natural adversities besetting the Middle East is found in the Book of Exodus. Seven calamities struck down the land of Egypt before the pharaoh agreed to let the Children of Israel depart. These plagues still stalk the land. Perhaps the greatest curse of all are mosquito-borne diseases. "And there came a grievous swarm of flies into the House of Pharaoh and into the servants' houses, and all the land of Egypt was corrupted by reason of the swarm of flies." Mosquitoes bear malaria, yellow fever, and other sicknesses that remain endemic. The riverine systems of Egypt and Iraq are particularly blighted by schistosomiasis, a disease that unfortunately spreads with the use of irrigation: a waterborne parasite enters via the bare soles of fieldworkers. Cattle diseases abound. So do locusts, which can swarm into highly cultivated areas where they may wipe out a large share of the year's crop.

Farmers also must contend with such man-made burdens as excessive or unfair taxation, governmental inefficiency and corruption, poor marketing facilities, the lack of rural credit, and deficiencies in transportation. In some regions land-holdings are small and scattered; modern plows, tractors, reaping machines, barbed-wire fences, and other such innovations cannot easily be introduced. Middle Eastern governments in Iran and Iraq, Egypt and Algeria, have attempted land reforms, but the redistribution of land to peasant farmers does not of itself raise agricultural productivity. Farmers require incentives in order to improve their methods. They need trucks and roads to transport their crops to the city; they need technical education, banking facilities, and veterinary and agricultural services; they require credit; they may need security of tenure, a proper handling of water rights—a complex physical and organizational infrastructure that cannot suddenly be improvised.

A Mixed Heritage

The world of the Middle East, whether pastoral or urban, has been overwhelmingly shaped by Islam. The Jews in Israel, the Maronite or Greek

Orthodox Christians in Lebanon, the Monophysite Copts in Egypt, and the Christian minorities in Syria and Iraq—these do not share in the Islamic legacy. But throughout the region as a whole Islam is the main cultural connecting link. We have made this point before, but it needs emphasis.

The Middle East, as we have also emphasized, shares a common legacy of Western colonialism. It is true that Turkey, Iran, and Afghanistan, although exposed to foreign invasion, have never been subject to direct colonial rule, but they have all experienced a great variety of military, political, cultural, and economic pressures from the West. Colonialism helped to determine the modern boundaries of such countries as Lebanon and Jordan; colonialism helped to diffuse Western technology and Western ideas. The latter reached the Middle East primarily through the use of the English and French languages which, while introducing modern science and technology, spread Western notions concerning democracy, popular sovereignty, the dialectical process in history, and the importance of class struggle.

In an economic sense, most Middle Eastern countries remain backward in comparison with the states of Western Europe. There are exceptions. The most advanced economy in the Middle East was established by the Jews in Israel and there are small modern enclaves in the surrounding Arab states. The oil sheikhdoms on the Persian Gulf have garnered enormous wealth from their exports and are among the world's bankers; Egyptian factories turn out some highly sophisticated products. Lebanon until recent years earned an international reputation as a center of trade, banking, and other financial services. But overall development has been uneven. The most powerful and prosperous Middle Eastern countries—Iran, Turkey, and Saudi Arabia—have a gross national product (GNP) less than that of Belgium and but a fraction of those of Great Britain or West Germany (table 2.1). There are striking inequalities in their respective resources. In 1977 the per capita income of Libya, a major oil-producing country, exceeded that of Japan and the USSR (in US dollars at market price, $4,440 as against $4,070 and $2,380, respectively); countries like Turkey and Algeria ranked just below Chile ($750 and $730 as against $830); the Sudan's per capita GNP was considerably less than that of a South African Bantustan ($380 as against $255).

Total agricultural and food production in North Africa and the Middle East rose faster than that of other developing regions between 1961 and 1972. North Africa, especially Algeria, did less well than most states in the Middle East. Yields in the Middle East are usually low, however. Only Egypt comes close to Western levels of productivity. High yields result from population growth, which brings larger markets and improved communications, and from the use of capital (irrigation raises yields and allows double cropping). More chemical fertilizers are now being employed, but at a rate that is still below the norm for Western Europe.

TABLE 2.1
Size and Productivity of Middle Eastern States
Compared to West Germany, Great Britain, and Belgium

Country	Population (thousands)	Estimated GNP in 1977 (thousand million $ US)
Algeria	18,420	10.1
Bahrein	345	1.7
Egypt	39,760	13.3
Iran	36,365	72.6
Iraq	12,470	16.3
Israel	3,700	14.2
Jordan	2,970	1.3
Kuwait	1,160	12.0
Lebanon	3,060	2.9
Libya	2,760	18.5
Morocco	18,590	9.5
Oman	837	2.5
Qatar	205	2.4
Saudi Arabia	7,730	55.4
Sudan	19,120	4.4
Syria	8,110	6.5
Turkey	42,110	46.6
Tunisia	6,250	5.0
United Arab Emirates	875	7.7
Yemen Arab Republic (North)	7,270	1.2
Yemen, People's Democratic Republic of (South)	1,830	0.22
West Germany	63,410	508.6
Great Britain	56,700	263.6
Belgium	9,930	73.4

Source: International Institute of Strategic Studies, *The Military Balance, 1978–1979* (London: The Institute, 1978).

North African and Middle Eastern agriculture has suffered from low output per agricultural worker (except in Israel) and low output per acre (except in Egypt, Israel, and Lebanon). This low level of output is due to poor climate (scarcity of rainfall), inefficient organization, and backward land tenure systems. Land reforms have been enacted and governments have supplied more agricultural credit and extension services, but with only relatively minor success. Only a few governments provide sufficient resources to significantly improve agricultural production. Most countries of the area invest more in manufacturing than they do in agriculture, since all seem foolishly determined to industrialize at all costs. Industrial developers hope to supply consumers with locally made goods in lieu of foreign imports, but the price of such import substitution policies is high. The new industries usually require a high degree of protection and their costs are frequently above world levels; consumers usually have to spend more on domestically produced products than on imported ones. Local consumers are also forced to pay higher taxes to subsidize the new industries. Hence import substitution, for all its political advantages, turns out to be retrograde in the economic sense. Nevertheless, these practices are likely to continue during the 1980s despite the costs that they entail for the consumer and, especially, for the farming community.

POLITICAL PROBLEMS

After Victor Emmanuel II, the great nineteenth-century Italian monarch, had helped to complete the unification of Italy, he said in a famous speech: "We have created Italy; now we have to create Italians." Many of the new Arab states are struggling in the same way to find their identity. Pan-Arab nationalism is of recent origin; it owes its development to the Western impact. Early modern nationalists, as we have explained, were frequently Christian Arabs—the first Westernized Arabs—who played a dominant part in intellectual life. Pan-Arabism rests on the belief that all Arabs are—or should be—one united people. Pan-Arabism is not, however, a cement sufficiently strong to hold the Arab states together.

It is not easy for Syrians or Iraqis to rally behind the banner of state nationalism. Accordingly, most Middle Eastern political movements attach to themselves the prestigious label of "revolution." The Middle East has experienced a plethora of coups and rebellions. There is also a long tradition of popular wars against foreigners; the Turkish campaign against Greece after World War I and the Algerian rising against the French after World War II are two examples. Under Kemal Atatürk's rule Turkey went through a national revolution; the Turks abandoned the religious seclusion of women, the supremacy of the Islamic religion, and even the Arabic alphabet. The creation of a Zionist state in Palestine was a traumatic experience of a different kind; immigrants of predominantly Western stock established a Western state within the Middle East. But no Arab state has passed through the equivalent of the French Revolution, which created a secular national identity that overrode regional and ethnic loyalties, and took its legitimacy from a notion of the public good that transcended sectional interests. Ties of kinship, friendship, and clientage remain powerful in the Middle East, more powerful than the links that bind men to great impersonal organizations—the state bureaucracy, the ruling party, the trade union. The military enjoy a strong position, and military coups are rife. But no Middle Eastern officer corps enjoys the corporate cohesion and the national prestige that fell to the officer corps in most states of nineteenth-century Europe.

Pan-Arabic creeds, strong from 1950 to 1970, have fallen into decline. Nasser was the natural leader of Pan-Arabism and Israel its enemy. But within the individual Arab states there is no consensus concerning the direction in which any particular country should move. Syrians and Iraqis oscillate between cooperation and hostility. Egyptians dispute among themselves whether their country could assert its "pharaonic" (i.e., indigenous) Egyptian identity or whether Egypt should regard itself primarily as an Islamic power, a Mediterranean country, or a revolutionary Afro-Arab state destined to head a great Arab coalition. Many Arab nationalists link the fate of the Middle East with Islam, but not all Arab nationalists are Muslims; Lebanese Christians were among the pioneers of secular Arab nationalism; Iraqi Kurds have played a considerable role in the Iraqi Communist Party. Israelis are equally divided. Some pin their faith to Judaism, others to various forms of secularism; most look upon themselves as Jews tied to a wider Jewish world; some want to be "Canaanites," rooted only to the soil of their native country.

Communalism and Nationalism

Throughout the Middle East, moreover, communalism remains strong, not merely in cultural and religious matters but in economic affairs. Some minority communities such as the highland Berbers, Maronites, Kurds, and Druzes, live in relatively well-defined areas. But others are widely dispersed. Many villages in various parts of the Middle East are composed of a major ethnic group and of minority groups who often provide specialists in particular occupations. Members of religious minority groups—Jews, Armenians, Copts, Maronites, Bahai, and others—have traditionally made up a large proportion of the indigenous entrepreneurs. Thus class struggles, as we explained in chapter 1, are overlaid with ethnoreligious conflicts. The predominance of communal loyalties in countries like Lebanon militates against compromise; politics all too often becomes a zero-sum game where one community's gain necessarily becomes another's loss. An aged Muslim on his deathbed decided to convert to Christianity—so goes a Lebanese joke. His family gathered around him, weeping. "How can you do such a dreadful thing, grandfather?" they asked. "Can't you see, my children," the old man answered, "I am dying—and then it will be one of them and not one of us!"

All too often, ethnosocial problems have been "solved" by the deliberate persecution and even destruction of religious minorities—the Armenians in the former Ottoman Empire, for instance, or the Assyrians in Iraq—or by the systematic expulsion of so-called aliens, as the Greeks were expelled from post–World War I Turkey and from the now Turkish-occupied zone of Cyprus, the European settlers from recently independent Algeria, the Jews from Iraq, and many Palestinians from Israel. These enforced population movements so familiar to the postwar Middle East are costly in economic terms. Cities like Algiers and Oran have suffered severely from the disappearance of the *pieds noirs* (European settlers); Alexandria shed its economic vitality with the departure of most Levantine Christians; Smyrna lost much of its prosperity when the Greeks were driven out—the list is long and melancholic. But such is the strength of communal loyalties that no Middle Eastern state has managed to create a sense of national feeling that transcends the force of communal bonds.

The problems of communalism are not by themselves insoluble. Christian and Muslim managed to coexist in the Lebanon for many years. Berber and Arab live side by side in Algeria and Morocco without constantly coming to blows. The problems of communalism, however, become aggravated when ethnic divisions coincide with class divisions, and when class divisions are exacerbated by militant ideologies that promise to create a new and better society. Christians in the Lebanon, especially the Maronites, were among the first to benefit from Western education, as were Jews, Copts, Greeks, and Armenians in various other parts of the Ottoman Empire. These minorities developed small elites of bankers, merchants, and entrepreneurs whose real or assumed wealth aroused both the religious prejudice and the cupidity of their less prosperous neighbors.

Economic development, far from reconciling the manifold quarrels between different ethnic groups, has often spawned new ethnic dissensions. In Saudi Arabia, for example, the stupendous development of the oil industry has created an ethnosocial pyramid. The leading military, clerical, diplomatic, and political positions have fallen to indigenous Saudis. Europeans and Americans fill many of the senior technical jobs; Syrians, Palestinians, Egyptians, and Pakistanis provide a considerable portion of the skilled workers, administrators, and teachers; immigrants from North and South Yemen fill most of the unskilled laboring jobs. As a French expert puts it: "No Saudi lays bricks or digs trenches; their social attitude, while common among the Western nations, is unhealthy and dangerous in a developing country like Saudi Arabia."[2]

The strength of communalism weakens political legitimacy and the weakening of legitimacy makes for political instability. At present, Israel alone in the Middle East remains a democratic state able to change its rulers through peaceful means. The Israeli army, though influential, is not an independent force in politics but is merely the Jewish electorate in arms. Other Middle Eastern regimes are subject to the threat of putsches, coups, and plots. Continuity remains to be established.

Sources of Instability

Why are Islamic states unstable? The short answer is that they lack legitimacy in the eyes of their people. Leaders, ruling structures, and ideologies command neither the universal respect nor the loyalty of their people. The problem of legitimacy is a complex one growing out of the history and culture of these new nations. It was worsened by European imperialism and by recent attempts at rapid modernization. Arabic, Turkish, and Iranian political systems have not developed a consensus on questions of identity, authority, social policy, ideology, and regional coordination. According to an Iraqi maxim, "You lick the hand you cannot bite."

Religion has divided the people and not united them. Sunnis oppose Shi'ites, secularists battle traditionalists for the souls of the people. Religious laws are based on the will of God as revealed in the Qur'an. All aspects of daily life—greetings, foods, manner of dress, customs and traditions—are governed by religion. This has meant that Islamic societies are often reluctant to change their customs because the latter are based on religion and on a way of life ordained by God and embodied in the Qur'an. Since social and political life are also under religious law, Islamic leaders, if they wish to gain public acceptance for modern policies and practices, must show how they conform to Islamic traditions and concepts.

Arab politics further suffer from the weakness of Arab political institutions. There has been an absence of sustained ideological commitment, of real revolutionary change. Arab politicians have been socially conservative and have practiced conspiratorial politics or military coups. The strength of Arab politics lies not so much in political parties or ideology as in the patron-client and family network. Arabs have seldom felt strong local nationalism, and Pan-Arab nationalism exists only insofar as it shares a common enemy—Israel.

The Middle East is also divided by militant ideologies: Marxism in various forms, Arab nationalism, and a militant Islamic revival that—ostensibly—looks to the past and to the pure ideals of the Qur'an. From Algeria and Egypt across Iran into Afghanistan, Islamic religious movements are on the upswing. The mullahs, imans, and ayatollahs widely, though not universally, believe that communists are materialistic and the West is decadent. The Iranian monarchy, once accepted by Western specialists as a modernizing force, recently fell to such a movement. The kings of Saudi Arabia and Jordan sit uneasily on their thrones. Turkey is in turmoil. Libya, subject to a militant Islamic dictatorship, has become a center of international terrorism; well financed, it is a million-dollar growth industry that gives employment not merely to gunmen but to a large supporting staff, one with good incomes and even pension plans.

Moderate forces are also at work. By the end of the 1970s, when the militant Arab socialist and nationalist creeds popular during the 1950s and 1960s were everywhere in decline, the blue-collar and white-collar workers, who were privileged compared with the rural poor, were gaining in influence—much to the militants' regret, since political debate increasingly turned from glory to the gross national product. Kinship and friendship groups remained the basic building blocks of Arab society; even Marxists could hold onto power only by manipulating extended networks of clientage and kinship. In countries like Egypt and Syria the prestige of bureaucratic management in the economy was on the decline. So was the reputation of state-run farms. Syria, Egypt, Algeria, Tunisia, having experimented during the 1960s with state or collective farms, all decided that production by individual landholders was more efficient. *Wasatiya* ("middle-ism"), a contemptuous term invented by Arab socialists for a halfway point between secularism and religion, has gained in influence as a philosophy of pragmatism applied to economic management and to foreign affairs.

The future of the Middle East will depend on how far these moderate forces can assert themselves against a militant Muslim revivalism that has captivated many members of the lower-middle class and the indigent farmers, and against various kinds of Marxism that are popular mainly among the intellectuals. Men of religion and the Qur'an command great respect. To the faithful the Qur'an is a record of God's purpose; to educated men it remains a precious cultural legacy. Marx and Engels, Lenin and Mao Tse-tung, are widely revered by students as prophets of a new creed of secular salvation. But few Middle Easterners have read Adam Smith, John Stuart Mill, or Milton Friedman. Much less do they cherish their principles. Marxists, however, remain split among themselves as do the Muslims, divided between Sunnis and Shi'ites.

Even in the great days of the Islamic religion, faith was never strong enough to act as a unifying bond between contending states. Today, Islamic countries continue to clash with each other and with their non-Islamic neighbors. Most Middle Eastern countries thus continue to be overarmed. Much poorer than the states of Western Europe, they proportionately spend far more on defense (table 2.2).

TABLE 2.2
COMPARATIVE DEFENSE EXPENDITURES OF CERTAIN MIDDLE EASTERN
AND WESTERN NATIONS, 1977

Country	Percentage of GNP Spent on Defense in 1977
Israel	29.9
Egypt (1974)	22.8
Syria	16.4
Jordan	11.5
Saudi Arabia	13.6
Iran	10.9
USSR	11.0/13.0
United States	6.0
South Africa	5.1
Great Britain	5.0
Germany	3.4

SOURCE: International Institute of Strategic Studies 1978, pp. 88–89.

Muslims versus Non-Muslims

Of all the conflicts that divide the Middle East, the confrontation between Israel and the Arab states is the most spectacular. Other Middle Eastern states clash over boundaries and oil claims, but Israel is the sole nation whose very survival is at stake. A protégé of the United States, it is locally regarded as a pariah state whose existence is an affront to its neighbors. Israel and Egypt, until recently adversaries, share problems that in some ways are strikingly similar: large and inefficient bureaucracies, deficit economies dependent on foreign handouts, and a form of military hypertrophy that induces each combatant to devote a major share of its GNP to defense expenditure. The effects of this military hypertrophy are aggravated by the cost of ultramodern weaponry. Mirage and Mig aircraft not only cost a great deal more than World War II Spitfires and Messerschmidts; they also need far more skilled pilots and mechanics and more expensive spare parts. The social and economic cost of such military investment is unbearably high for poverty-stricken countries and it continues to rise.

The Arab-Israeli struggle is only one among many between Muslims and non-Muslims. There are other conflicts along what might be considered the frontiers of Islam. Turks and Greeks clash over Cyprus and over many of the Aegean islands adjoining the shore of Asia Minor. Muslim Arabs sympathize with Muslim Somalis and Eritreans who battle against Ethiopia, a non-Muslim state now subject to a Marxist dictatorship. In the Sudan, the Muslim northerners hold down a non-Muslim majority. In Chad, Christians and pagans clash with Muslims. To make matters worse, there are bitter dissensions between various Muslim states themselves. Iraq has invaded Iran. Algeria and Morocco are at odds, as are North and South Yemen. Hostility against Israel provides a rallying cry for the majority of Arabs, but President Sadat's peace initiative has turned even the Israeli issue into a source of bitter disagreement within the Arab community—notwithstanding all the hopes for the unification of the Arab world. No great leader has arisen to take Nasser's place as the head of Pan-Arabism. While Pan-Arabism will hardly be a strong force in the 1980s, Pan-Islamic creeds are likely to make a much more powerful impact as people turn back to older values and religion. The Arab world might well be torn by more Khomeini-type revolutions in the future.

ECONOMIC PROBLEMS

The Middle East, as we have said, is economically backward. The reasons for this are complex. Many Arab nationalists blame the weaknesses of their societies on the real or alleged sins of Western colonialists. But the Western intrusion was more an effect than a cause. It was made possible because, even before World War I, the deficiencies of the precolonial regimes in countries like Tunisia, Morocco, and Egypt invited the breakup of the existing Islamic monarchies.

For reasons that are much disputed, the great Islamic kingdoms as well as Southern Italy and the Balkan Peninsula, once leaders in world civilization, fell behind in the race for scientific and industrial advancement. As we have indicated, this process began during the sixteenth and seventeenth centuries and accelerated during the subsequent century and a half. The military power of the Islamic states decayed. The Islamic world shared to but a minor extent in the industrial, commercial, and agricultural revolutions that transformed Western and Central Europe.

Some progress there was, but its impact was uneven in extent and in time. As a generalization, it can be said that the economies of the Middle East have passed through a number of distinct—though interconnected—stages whose onset varied from country to country and from region to region. The economies initially were fragmented into clusters of villages and kinship groupings; though linked by tenuous networks of trade, they were mainly self-sufficient. There commonly was a balance between sedentary agriculture, pastoral farming of a nomadic kind, and small-scale craft industries that often hinged on market towns and administrative centers.

The gradual infusion of Western goods, machine-made and cheap, and of Western thought and of Western arms helped to change the old order, as did the extension of roads, the construction of railways, the spread of Western schools and newspapers. Rulers like Muhammad Ali in Egypt (c. 1769–1849) tried to create a modern industry by inviting in French technicians but, being short of skilled manpower, capital, and other technological resources, did not get far with these developments. The Middle East lacked the economic structures and political institutions that had facilitated the rise of modern manufactures in eighteenth-century and nineteenth-century England. Neither were there easily accessible deposits of coal and iron of the kind essential to the West's Industrial Revolution. The bulk of indigenous capital in the Middle East went into trade and money lending, and into land used primarily to produce Egyptian cotton for export.

Industrial development on a large scale came relatively late, though it was far from insignificant. In Egypt, for example, manufacturers received some encouragement during World War I and a much bigger boost in World War II. Development after that was rapid; factories—particularly textile mills—opened in Egypt, Lebanon, Syria, and Iraq. The speed of industrial development was impressive in some sectors; so was the ability of Egyptian industries to turn to sophisticated manufactures. During the late 1960s progress was virtually stopped by war and war preparations, yet by the early 1970s Egypt had achieved a per capita income of $220 a year, almost three times that of India.

A great deal of Middle Eastern manufacturing is concerned with agricultural processing (sugar, tobacco), petroleum products, construction (cement), textiles, paper, and such light industrial commodities as furniture. Industry for the most part lags far behind agriculture as a source of income. In most parts of the Middle East agricultural yields remain low, though the potential is sometimes great. Transportation facilities and markets are so inadequate that farmers cannot easily improve or market their yields.

The Impact of Oil

From the international standpoint, no single commodity can compare with oil. The petroleum industry in such countries as Iran, Saudi Arabia, and Kuwait was created by Western enterprise. By the late 1970s, the Islamic countries between them accounted for more than half the total oil production within the noncommunist world (table 2.3). The Persian Gulf alone provides at present some 71 percent of Western European oil needs. The producer countries' revenues from oil have been invested in refineries, factories, ports, and many other enterprises. Between 1974 and 1978 alone, the governments of the Organization of Petroleum Exporting Countries (OPEC) enjoyed revenues, largely derived from foreign trade, amounting to $550 billion; an estimated $500 billion had been spent on goods, services, and military expenditures.[3]

Western Europe, Japan, and to a lesser extent the United States rely on

TABLE 2.3
WORLD CRUDE OIL PRODUCTION, EXCLUDING NATURAL GAS LIQUIDS, 1977

Source	Oil (1,000 barrels per day)
WORLD	53,480
Noncommunist world	46,570
United States	14,010
Saudi Arabia	9,200
Iran	5,660
Kuwait	1,970
Iraq	2,330
United Arab Emirates	2,010
Qatar	430
Oman	340
Syria	180
Other Middle Eastern countries, excluding Africa	110
Libya	2,080
Algeria	1,040
Egypt	420
ISLAMIC COUNTRIES (combined)	25,580

SOURCE: *International Energy Statistical Review*, October 31, 1979, p. 1.

Middle Eastern oil for their prosperity. Their dependence on Middle Eastern imports has caused an economic revolution that has raised the oil producers to the rank of Great Powers whose commercial strength far exceeds their military, industrial, and diplomatic significance. Middle Eastern oil as a source of apparently illimitable wealth can be compared to the gold and silver once carried by sailing ships from the New World to Spain.

But economic development has proved to be both a blessing and a curse. As table 2.1 shows, the impact of oil has created bizarre discrepancies of wealth in the Middle East. The GNP of a tiny state like Oman with less than one million people is, in statistical terms, nearly as large as that of Algeria with a population of more than eighteen million. Social tensions within the oil-producing states have been accentuated. Agriculture is widely neglected. In Iran, for instance, agricultural production dropped from 18 percent of GNP in 1973 to 8 percent in 1977; food imports during the same period rose in value from $32 million to $1.5 thousand million. Inflation is rampant throughout the area. Many traditional industries and traditional pursuits have declined. In Saudi Arabia the nomadic population now amounts to only some seven hundred thousand out of seven million people. Within a decade the nomadic way of life will probably have disappeared altogether—a serious matter in a kingdom that claims to be built on traditional Arab values. There have been great shifts in population; three million out of the seven million inhabitants of Saudi Arabia are probably immigrants; they include Yemenites, Egyptians, Sudanese, Chadians, Pakistanis, Palestinians, Syrians, Lebanese, and others. The cities increased in an explosive fashion. Riyadh, the capital of Saudi Arabia and once a sleepy township, now has some seven hundred fifty thousand inhabitants; their number may soon pass the million mark.

Much of the oil revenue has been poorly spent. According to a leading expert, Walter J. Levy, the actual value received by the OPEC countries for their purchases abroad may have been no more than half the nominal value. Too large a percentage of OPEC revenue has been utilized for military purchases, for prestige projects, and for the purpose of maintaining swollen bureaucracies. At the same time, the operation and maintenance of ports, transportation, hospitals, and schools, the provision of sewerage and water for the fast-growing cities, and the support of a welfare economy have become an ever-increasing budgetary drain at a time when inflation, in many Middle Eastern countries, is unrestrained.

Oil, moreover, is an irreplaceable form of wealth. Unless the Middle Eastern countries can create viable economies with sound agricultural foundations, a number of the OPEC countries may find themselves in perilous condition once the existing oil wealth has petered out. They could share the fate of sixteenth-century Spain, which wasted the gold and silver from its Latin American empire.

SOCIOECONOMIC PROBLEMS

The Middle East has been changing—and will change—on a scale unprecedented in its history. In many ways the condition of its peoples has improved in a spectacular fashion. The last decade or so has seen a striking increase in production and in the number of persons employed. Life expectancy has gone up; living standards have risen. Millions of Turks, Iranians, and Arabs have acquired new skills: sons of peasants and herdsmen now work as financial experts, test pilots, industrial chemists, hydroelectrical engineers, factory managers, or computer specialists. They bear not the slightest resemblance to the childish stereotypes of turbaned, gun-wielding, teeth-gnashing, Middle Eastern terrorists that fill so many cartoons in Western newspapers.

But in social terms, development has entailed a substantial debit column. In all Middle Eastern countries population growth has soared, reaching a rate of between 2.1 percent a year in Egypt and 3.4 percent in Syria. This demographic expansion has been accompanied by rapid and often unmanageable urbanization. Cairo in 1975 had over eight million people; today it has nearly ten million. Tehran and its satellite cities contain five million people; the population of Damascus is approaching two million. Many of the urban newcomers live in shanty towns ill provided with water, electricity, and sewerage facilities.

In most Middle Eastern countries the birthrate remains high. The population contains more and more young people. The resulting demographic shifts contribute to cultural instability, to problems of education, to crime, to an insufficiency of jobs for school dropouts, and to the radicalization of unemployed or underemployed youngsters. The urban work force has grown, but too many workers lack skills; their employment often depends on short-lived construction booms and on a fluctuating demand for menial labor. Agricultural development, on the other hand, has frequently been neglected, a serious omission in countries where, as in Syria and Egypt, farming remains the primary industry.[4] The policy of favoring the city over the village makes no sense in an area where malnutrition is a serious problem and where farming methods remain backward; nevertheless, it is hard to persuade townbred planners in mainly agricultural countries that rural development should come first.

How will these problems be solved? Middle Easterners overwhelmingly look to the intervention of the state, by which they understand either an Islamic republic or some form of socialist commonwealth. The widespread faith in state direction originally owed little to the prescriptions of Marx and Lenin and more, perhaps, to Arab communalism and to dislike of such ethnic minorities as the Jews, Greeks, Armenians, and Lebanese, who frequently supplied the original cadres of the bourgeoisie. Statist traditions were strengthened by Western rule. The Western colonial officials, like earlier rulers of indigenous origin, created public works and interfered in the local economies in many ways. The impact of war further strengthened the powers of the state. During World War II, for instance, the Allies set up the Middle East Supply Center through which they exercised comprehensive control over imports, exports, and investments.

The successor states took over these traditions of government intervention. There was no substantial class of indigenous manufacturers or businessmen. The expansion of university education created a supply of graduates who looked for employment to public service in state and party bureaucracies and in state-run corporations, with the result that planning, control, interference, and ownership by the state became part of an economic credo that now prevails throughout most of the Middle East. This faith easily coexists with socioreligious prejudices concerning the supposed "materialism," "heartlessness," and "irreligion" of the West. To this day, science and technology, business, banking, and management have never commanded the respect accorded to public administration, defense, and government.

The bulk of investment capital, then, has gone into public enterprise. The private sector has profited little from development plans that favor an oddly assorted alliance of foreign investors and bureaucrats employed in state enterprises. The bureaucracies themselves draw their candidates from the swollen student population. Iran, for instance, now has about a hundred thousand university students and has more than a half-million students in secondary or more advanced institutions; seventy thousand Iranian students live abroad. Many of these students experienced corruption in the examination system. They are frequently disillusioned by Marxist propaganda or by the need for the personal "pull" required for official advancement. The bureaucracies in countries as diverse as Israel, Egypt, and Iran have grown unwieldy, unyielding, interfering, often corrupt, and inefficient. Above all, they have grown. In Iran the government at the time of the 1979 coup maintained more than eight hundred thousand civil servants. However, barely half of their jobs had any social utility. The country employs in addition over a million people in government-owned or government-subsidized industries. These bureaucratic bodies still provide a great number of sinecures but leave their incumbents dispirited with useless work and their clients angry at public inefficiency and red tape—a striking contrast with the superior working morale and competent management of multinational corporations.

Not surprisingly, Western capitalism is widely disliked or envied. The oil wealth of the Middle East was originally developed by the infusion of Western capital, technology, and enterprise. Most Middle Easterners believe that foreign investors did not deserve the profits they got and that the Middle East has been grossly exploited. Arab socialists and conventional Marxists alike look to public rather than private enterprise. Private enterprise remains identified with the West, and anti-Western sentiment remains strong among both Marxists and militant Muslims. Muslims and Marxists in Iran blame the real or alleged iniquities committed by the shah and his followers on Western backers. In Algeria radical revolutionaries gained widespread popular support only when they stopped talking about an Algerian Algeria and professed to fight against French unbelievers for a Muslim Algeria. Jordanians, Egyptians, and Algerians all evince bitter hatred toward the state of Israel, regarded variously as either the puppet of the West or its secret puppet master.

These are some of the realities that face American statesmanship. Only a genius would be able to deal with them in a manner likely to meet with success. The United States must be concerned that other oil-rich countries do not follow the Iranian example. Although their situations are not exactly analogous, other traditional societies in the Middle East face similar problems—too much money, too rapid modernization, and a weak central government.

THE FUTURE IN THE MIDDLE EAST

The Middle Eastern and North African economies can become more viable in the 1980s than they are at present provided the countries in question can live at peace, reduce their oversized armaments, limit their huge bureaucracies, maintain a tolerant policy toward their religious and ethnic minorities, improve their skills, save at a higher rate than at present, and solve their foreign exchange problems. In general they need to spend more on their agricultural sectors and pay more attention to farmers' requirements. The big problems of the 1980s in the Middle East will be population and food. Countries will increasingly be unable to feed their people or to provide work for them.

Inflation and the flight to towns has resulted in slums, overcrowding, and lower living standards. Farms are deserted, so agricultural productivity is down and food imports have increased. Foreign workers and technicians are brought in to run the new and modern industries and schools and to service electronic and military equipment. All the oil states are spending huge sums on arms. Middle Eastern countries generally disburse too much money on munitions and the local economies have not been able to absorb the sums disbursed. With building booms, local services have been outstripped. Inflation and new wealth have led to excessive government spending and imports.

Rapid development programs, when combined with this great wealth, have weakened traditional values and social systems. Middle Eastern societies stand between two worlds, the old and the new, but belong to neither. Rapid change has led naturally to frustrations and resentments and these are often used as excuses for attacking the government or the foreigner in the nation's midst.

Unfortunately, few Middle Eastern states are in a position to modernize or effectively to diversity their economies. Islamic states have many burdens: poor leaders, unskilled labor, a difficult climate (too much heat and too little water), poor soils, and the survival of backward traditions and social customs. These are not unsurmountable obstacles, but no ready-made solutions are in sight.

Prospects for Economic Growth

What can we expect for the Middle East in the 1980s? According to a 1978 Rand Corporation study by Arthur Smithies, during the 1980s the oil-rich Arab countries—Saudi Arabia, Kuwait, Iraq, and Libya—will grow quite rapidly because of their increased revenues from oil sales.[5] Saudi Arabia will be the leader because of its willingness to import foreign labor and technology. By 1985, however, even the Saudis will have balance-of-payment problems and will have to slow down their development plans. Iraq and Iran will have to cope with the problems engendered by war. Oil-poor states such as Egypt, Jordan, and Syria will grow only if they continue to receive economic aid.

After 1985 the Arabs will probably experience trouble in transforming their economies, even with oil wealth. Capital shortages are only one factor in economic growth. Inflation and balance-of-payment problems will be the most serious handicaps to development. Imports of foreign commodities, labor, and skills will outstrip export revenues. Even if countries like Saudi Arabia expand production and increase prices, they will have problems in paying for their development plans. The oil-rich then will drop back to moderate economic growth rates of 5 to 7 percent. Kuwait is already pursuing a cautious and conservative development program. The oil-poor states will continue through the 1980s to be a drain on the wealthy, but since the security of these nations, rich or poor, depends on friendly neighbors, the rich ones will continue to pay out aid.

Egypt   In demographic terms, by far the most powerful Arab state is Egypt. About 30 percent of all Arab-speaking people in the world live in Egypt; Egypt commands the greatest reservoir of skilled labor and managerial skills in the Arab world; the Egyptian army is the most powerful of all Arab forces; no anti-Israeli coalition would get very far without Egyptian military support. Since the end of the 1973 war against Israel, Egypt has made a remarkable recovery. (By the end of 1979, Egypt's annual economic growth rate stood at about 9 percent, as against zero at the end of hostilities.) Nevertheless, Egypt is likely to face a host of troubles. It must contend with diminishing land resources and a growing population. Its oil supplies are modest; there is little in the country to attract foreign investors, but much bureaucratic red tape to discourage them. If the Egyptian government can limit population growth, reduce its foreign exchange deficits by improving exports, end government subsidies, tighten credit, and reduce the money supply, Egypt has a chance. If President Sadat can put his economic house in order and continue to receive generous foreign aid, Egypt might return to its healthy pre-1967 growth rate.

Syria, helped by aid from Arab countries, had an economic growth rate of 12 percent from 1973 to 1976, but probably will fall back to 5 or 6 percent during the 1980s. Jordan is aiming at 12 percent, but owing to its scanty resources, inflation, and labor shortages it will be lucky to reach 5 or 6 percent.

Iraq and the other oil-rich states   Among the oil-rich states, the leading Arab country during the 1980s may well be Iraq. It has a good balance between physical size and population, oil and agricultural resources, while its development plans are more modest and realistic than the Saudis'. It does, however, face two major challenges to its stability and leadership role in the 1980s. The Ba'athist government is Sunni but rules a Shi'ite population that knows of events in Iran. The Ba'ath Party is essentially an Arab-Marxist secular movement, and will have to placate the Shi'ite religious leaders.* The second threat to Iraqi leadership will come from the small but well-organized Iraqi Communist Party, which has roots among Kurds and poor Shi'ites.

Iraq, like all other socialist states, has had an inefficient, large bureaucracy and its people have been underproductive. Development has been impeded by shortages of labor, expertise, and material. But there are signs of improvement. New land reclamation projects promise to end food imports. Libya, on the other hand, has ceased to grow economically; oil apart, its resources are scanty and its government has a poor record in economic management.

For oil-producing states, shortages of capital will not be a constraint on development. Since they earn vast amounts of foreign currency, they will be able to buy and to use immediately a large amount of advanced technology. If they can learn to manage their resources—or can have others manage them—they will be able to reach a very high rate of growth. Iran, Iraq, and Algeria have sufficient population, natural resources, and human resources to develop at a rate of 9 to 10 percent a year. Whether this rate is attained will depend, of course, on whether the area enjoys peace, political stability, and reasonable governance. Kuwait has done quite well under competent leadership. But other oil-producing countries such as Saudi Arabia, Libya, the United Arab Emirates, and Qatar face a harder challenge. Even though their capital supply is enormous, their populations are small; they also lack water and other natural resources. They have few trained people, backward agricultures, and little or

---

* After the fall of the shah and the return of Khomeini, Ba'athist leaders were to be seen frantically visiting mosques and religious shrines.

no industry or infrastructure. The harsh climate wears out men, machinery, and structures. However, Charles Issawi has observed that capital and technology can overcome even these difficulties if the Islamic conservatives and incompetent planners do not intrude.[6]

The oil-poor states For states other than the major oil producers—Morocco, Tunisia, Egypt, Sudan, Israel, Jordan, Syria, the two Yemens, and Turkey—the future is likely to be more difficult. All of them are paying more for the goods they import than for those they export. They depend on aid, grants, and capital from outside. The economies of Israel and Turkey may continue to grow at 5 to 6 percent per annum, but their exports are declining and their military costs rising. Egypt, Morocco, Tunisia, and the Sudan, with good agricultural sectors, should grow at a reasonable rate, provided population pressures do not consume the increase in productivity and government mismanagement is reduced.

The 1980s: A North-South Dialogue?

Can the Middle Eastern and North African economies become viable in the 1980s? In theory, they might be successful, but their planners face a hard task. They have to train technicians, managers, and administrators to run modern states and modern economies. In numerical terms, this seems possible. In 1971, Arab college and university students numbered four hundred thousand; by 1981 they will probably number twice that. Iran, Israel, and Turkey also have an expanding student population. Unfortunately, as we have said, technical, managerial, and commercial skills do not, in these areas, command the prestige accorded to governmental and academic attainments. The Middle Eastern countries will have to save at a high rate—at least 20 to 25 percent of GNP—to finance new investments. This rate is less than the 30 to 35 percent attained by several Asian countries. Yet, faced with heavy military expenditure and heavy outlays on swollen bureaucracies and costly prestige projects, few Middle Eastern countries will reach adequate rates of investment.

The Middle Eastern countries must also seek to reduce existing trade deficits. They can do this by the export either of goods or of services, including money sent home from abroad by migrant workers, services provided to tourists, and other such actions. Oil-producing states will have to diversify their economies so that they can continue to make a living when the precious fuel runs out. Proven reserves vary from twenty to eighty years, though potential reserves are probably greater than the proven ones. Above all, the Middle Eastern countries, without exception, must devote their resources to agricultural development, paying more attention to the needs of the farmer than they do at present.

Few Middle Eastern states will develop at any great speed during the

1980s; on the contrary, they are to face further troubles. Prophecies are always risky, but there is no likelihood at present that from the Middle Eastern states will evolve what two more optimistic authors have called a "cohesive, cooperative, regional development strategy or collective bargaining position in relation to the North."[7] Because of their economic differences and rivalries, various Middle Eastern states will fail to cooperate regionally, and bilateral networks will predominate.

The oil-rich should increase their distance from the oil-poor and will largely ignore the needs of their neighbors—except to ensure the continued dependency of poorer states. There will be no federation of the poor South against the richer North, nor will the richer states in the area do much to help the poorer states. Oil power will not be used to force the North to invest in the South and help to develop it. The poor, then, may well get poorer and the rich richer.

The ruling elites of the Middle East have no strategy for a North-South dialogue. The oil boycott of 1973 was against Israel and her allies; it did not represent an effort to obtain economic benefits for the South as a whole. A North-South dialogue there will be in the 1980s, but the South will not be able to overcome regional differences and inequalities in order to present a united front against the North.

Pan-Arab unity has been shattered; no individual state is willing to sacrifice its interests for the ideals of Pan-Arabism. The rich do not want economic integration; the weak and divided fear absorption into larger units. Saudi Arabia wants economic clients, not independent, self-reliant allies. The Saudis will try to perpetuate the dependence on them of Egypt or the Sudan; they will not give or lend Egypt large sums to transform its economy. Collective action for the Middle Eastern states' economic advancement has proven impossible except over the issue of oil. Middle Eastern states, in other words, are unequal in resources and divided in politics and policies; they will not present a united front to the North. Instead they will continue to bargain bilaterally for favors from the North.

The future, then, is not bright for most countries of the Middle East. It is even darker if one adds the problems caused by the Arab-Israeli dispute. A solution that will protect Israel and meet the legitimate needs of Palestinians is therefore essential for the region as a whole, as is an Iraqi-Iranian peace.

Given these difficulties, only an optimist would look to a bright future. But the Middle East has confounded many prophets of woe, and the future may yet turn out to be happier than the past.

3

Trouble Spots: I.
The Maghreb, Israel,
and Lebanon

We Americans tend to be businesslike and oriented toward problem solving; we seek solutions—and stability. In the Middle East, neither may be possible. We must learn, in the 1980s, to live with instability, and with the insolubility of some problems. Furthermore, we should not see the Middle East only through the lens of the Arab-Israeli dispute; the area has innumerable other problems and tensions. There is poverty to be overcome; there is excessive population growth; there are backward peoples to be educated and made healthy; there is agriculture to be improved. In the following two chapters we will discuss some of the major problem countries, regions, and issues.

THE MAGHREB

The Maghreb (Maghrib), the western portion of the Islamic world, is commonly included in the "Near East." In fact, though, Morocco is no further from the United States than is Spain; Libya is no more distant from America than is Germany. The Maghreb covers a huge area: Morocco, Tunisia, and Algeria, with Libya adjoining. It is a region extraordinarily varied in its geographic and ethnographic features, yet with certain other features in common. The modern state system of the Maghreb comes from its colonial background. Roughly three-quarters of the population speak Arabic as their mother tongue; most of the remainder use Berber. A knowledge of French, the language of yesterday's rulers in Morocco, Tunisia, and Algeria, is common among the Muslim middle classes and intelligentsia of these countries. Italian

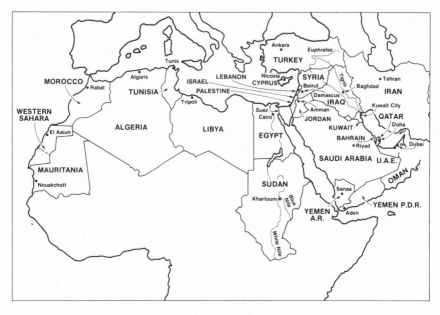

FIGURE 3.1 THE MAGHREB

is widely understood in Libya and Spanish in parts of northern Morocco and in what used to be the Spanish Sahara.

The population distribution, due to geographical conditions, is uneven. Vast stretches of North Africa consist of uninhabitable wasteland, mountain country, or desert; the fertile, densely populated regions might be likened to islands set in the desert, or placed between the desert and the sea. The urban population continues to rise at a rapid rate; nearly half the population of Algeria and Tunisia and nearly a third of Morocco's live in towns. Agriculture for the most part remains backward, yet the farmers are expected to produce food for an ever-growing number of mouths while official policies favor industry, the bureaucracy, and the armed forces over the needs of the farming community.

Algeria

Maghreb countries differ in population and size (table 3.1). Their GNP remains low and a considerable proportion of it is spent on defense. The largest North African state is Algeria. French colonizers, only a small proportion of whom were owners of large estates, unified the area, reclaimed swamp and desert, laid the foundations of Algeria's logistic infrastructure, and created an export-oriented agricultural economy that depended mainly on small-scale and medium-range agricultural enterprise. The Algerian revolution led to the country's independence from France in 1962 at the cost of heavy loss of life, widespread property destruction, the expulsion of some eight hundred thousand Europeans, and the establishment of a tightly structured one-party state with a parasitic bureaucracy.

The ruling party, known as the Front de Libération Nationale (FLN), enjoys a monopoly of power. It derives its legitimacy from having led the long and bloody struggle for independence against the French; it aims at creating a socialist order, neutralist in orientation, dedicated to the "mobilization of the masses." In practice, the new order rests on state capitalism run by a new class of party functionaries, bureaucrats, and ideologues, with worker participation in industrial management and state control over key positions within the economy. In 1966 the state nationalized the mines, the lands formerly owned by Europeans, and insurance companies. The state took over most of the country's banking operations and it now runs the mining and petroleum industries. These latter are major assets in a country that holds great resources of oil, natural gas, iron, uranium, zinc, copper, coal, salt, and other minerals—many as yet untouched. The government also embarked on a large-scale industrial development program including steel installations, iron foundries, phosphate processing plants, petrochemical industries, and the manufacture of vehicles. The government's land reform schemes reduced the size of the few large estates, set up cooperatives, and instituted "socialist villages" on nationalized lands.

The FLN has had substantial success in expanding the economy and in giving Algerians a new pride in their achievements. But unemployment remains high. Tens of thousands of Algerians go to France to work, while agriculture remains neglected. Over half Algeria's domestic work force stays on the land, yet farming contributes only 7.3 percent of the gross domestic product

TABLE 3.1
THE MAGHREB

	Algeria	Libya	Mauritania	Morocco	Tunisia
Area (in 1,000 sq. km.)	2,318	1,760	1,031	447	185
Population (est. 1977, in 1,000)	20,340	3,060	1,161 (1970)	18,240	7,840
GNP at market prices (in million $ US)	$16,060	$16,000	$460	$9,220	$4,790
Urban population (percent, 1975)	49.9%	30.5%	11.1%	38.0%	46.9%
GNP per capita ($ US, 1976)	$990	$1,070	$340	$540	$840
Average annual real growth (percent, 1970–1975)	4.3%	3.9%	2.6%	3.0%	6.9%

SOURCE: *Middle East Yearbook* (London: IC Magazine, 1979), pp. 64–65.

(GDP). Foodstuffs account for a quarter of Algeria's import bill, but the 1974–1977 plan allocated little more than 15 percent to agricultural development and water projects. Meanwhile land reform has run into numerous snags. Algeria, moreover, is heavily in debt—so heavily that debt servicing is expected to reach about 25 percent of the total value of its exports by 1985. On the other hand, oil exports have enabled Algeria to improve its international trading position. The country has ceased to be economically dependent on France; by 1977 the United States had replaced France as Algeria's principal trading partner. The economic rapprochement has been accompanied by a more moderate course in domestic and in foreign politics that has modified Algeria's formerly intransigeant line.

Morocco

Algeria's North African rival is Morocco, a country whose problems are in many ways similar. Morocco, like Algeria, has a high rate of population growth. Between 1960 and 1977 the number of people went up by 25 percent; agricultural production, however, increased by no more than 10 percent. Urban unemployment and rural underemployment remain major social problems. In addition, Morocco has to contend with a large landless rural population. In 1961 one-third of the people in the countryside owned no land at all, and many Moroccans who do own land can barely live off it. In 1973, 88 percent of all landowners held less than 10 hectares.

There are some striking political differences between Algeria and Morocco. Algeria is mainly an Arab country, while about 40 percent of the Moroccan population consists of Berbers, a primarily rural people. Algeria owes its existence as a nation to French colonization; Morocco was only a French protectorate. The Moroccan monarchy assumed an active part in the struggle against French overlordship and retains a substantial measure of popular support. Algeria is a one-party state; Morocco permits several political parties to operate. Algerian economic development centers on a large state sector that favors industry, including heavy industry; the Moroccans give priority to light industries, tourism, and agriculture linked to large irrigation schemes. Algeria takes pride in a "militant" foreign policy that stresses—at least formally—Algeria's community of interests with the Third World. Morocco prefers to cooperate more with France and with the United States, going as far as giving a cautious welcome to President Sadat's original peace initiative in 1977 while encouraging Jewish emigrants to return from Israel to Morocco.

The two countries have clashed bitterly over a number of territorial issues. The most serious of these concerns the fate of the former Spanish Sahara. In 1975 Spain agreed to withdraw from the Spanish Sahara, while Morocco and Mauritania agreed to partition the Spanish Sahara between them. The new settlement, however, aroused bitter opposition from the POLISARIO (Popular Front for the Liberation of Sequiet el-Hamra and Rio de Oro), an Algerian-backed guerrilla organization that claimed to represent the territory's hundred thousand or so nomads. The POLISARIO's demand for an independent Saharan state led to heavy fighting, and Mauritania suffered the most from the consequences. Its shaky economy was nearly wrecked and, to make matters worse, Senegal began to put forward territorial claims to Mauritania's fertile southern territory. In the end, Mauritania withdrew from the struggle and Morocco took over the former Mauritanian sector of the disputed Western Sahara.

But Morocco's struggle became increasingly hard. The POLISARIO formations—highly mobile, well equipped with Soviet-made surface-to-air missiles, rocket launchers, and automatic weapons—began to outgun the Moroccan forces. By the end of 1979 US aid began to increase; the Moroccans' fighting efficiency improved as they grew more skilled in coordinating land and air operations against their elusive foe. Nevertheless, Morocco continued to face a difficult position. War entailed serious economic deprivation as well as a constant need to keep up with Algeria's armed forces, well supplied as they were by the Soviet Union. The Organization for African Unity (OAU) split over the Western Sahara issue, but by the middle of 1980, the forty-nine member states of the OAU had agreed to recognize the newly formed "Sahrawi Arab Democratic Republic." The Arab states likewise were unable to reach agreement over the issue, with the Arab League and the gulf states generally supporting Morocco's line. United States policy towards Morocco lacked any kind of strategic sense. Morocco, a moderate Arab state, controls the Strait of Gibraltar, one of the world's most important waterways. Morocco had followed a pro-Western policy, yet the United States refused its support to Morocco over the Western Saharan issue. It was only in May 1979 that US diplomacy recognized the importance of Morocco and the Sudan, and sought to keep them in the ranks of moderate Afro-Arab states.

Morocco has been an important force in restraining radical Arab states and in facilitating Egyptian-Israeli peace talks. The United States needs to keep Morocco and the Sudan as supporters of Sadat and not to let them join the radical "rejectionist" bloc. Saudi Arabia, which supports the Sudan much as it had helped to provide financial aid to Egypt, is the key country pressuring both King Hassan and President Numeiri to cut their ties with Egypt. A US mission was sent in May to offer more aid and help to the Sudan and Morocco. Morocco requires military equipment to fight the POLISARIO in the western Sudan; Hassan specifically needs OV-10 counterinsurgency aircraft, advanced helicopter gunships, sensors for night engagements, and other military hardware. Morocco has now received some of this equipment, but continues to call for more arms. The United States in its own interest should continue to help

Morocco while encouraging Moroccan-Algerian negotiations for a compromise solution.

The Carter administration criticized Morocco for civil rights violations, though Morocco had a better record on civil rights than Algeria or Libya. Morocco has a relatively free press, permits opposition parties, and is ruled by a constitutional monarch. We should help Hassan against the POLISARIO and ignore—for the time being—claims to self-determination for scattered and ethnically heterogeneous nomad communities that lack the wherewithal to set up a viable state.

The sultan's throne is by no means secure. Sultan Hassan is a traditionalist who depends on a religious and military elite; in effect, though, he governs alone. He tries to do too much himself and is afraid to share power. The society is split between Arabic- and Berber-speakers, and the army is dominated by the Berbers. Hassan—or at least the royal family—is criticized for corruption, inefficiency, and ostentatious living while 60 percent of the population remain in the backward, barter-oriented sector of the economy. But the monarchy also has distinct assets, including the advantage of past association with the anti-colonial cause. Hassan is a more skillful ruler than the erstwhile shah of Iran, and his foreign policy, aiming at the incorporation of what used to be the northern part of Spanish Sahara, is popular.

It is in America's interest that monarchical rule of a moderate nature should continue to prevail and that a friendly rather than a radical power should control the Strait of Gibraltar. The United States has used Moroccan territory for airbases and communications; it may need to do so again. An unstable or an unfriendly Morocco could hurt the interests of Israel, Egypt, and Zaïre. Moroccan troops have twice saved Mobutu of Zaïre from losing the cobalt-rich and copper-rich Shaba Province. Five thousand troops keep Zaïre in the Western camp. Morocco has been a moderate voice in Middle Eastern politics and Hassan's support is necessary for our efforts to make the Egyptian-Israeli peace treaty work. Only ignorant congressmen, a weak State Department, and an incompetent president could justify selling helicopters to President Qaddafi (al-Quaddafi, Khadafy, Gaddafy) of Libya while refusing such hardware to King Hassan. US support for Hassan can counter Libya's massive buildup of Soviet arms, which threatens NATO's control of the Mediterranean.

Libya

Libya is both the poorest and the richest country in the Maghreb. Rocky wastelands and deserts cover most of the territory; there are no rivers; fertile land is confined to a few oases and the coastal plain. In relation to Libya's huge area, its population is small—just over three million, according to the

1978 census. Farming standards generally remain low, even though the majority of Libyans make their living from arable or pastoral farming (Libyans have to import food to cover the deficit). The country, however, also has great assets. Vast underground reserves of water have recently been discovered at Kufra; these have widened the scope for irrigation, increasing crop yields to such an extent that Libya might become self-sufficient in food by the early 1980s. At the same time, modern techniques of "sand fixing" (stabilizing shifting sand dunes) and reafforestation may improve the country's ecological balance. Still more important, Libya has become a major oil producer; between 1970 and 1977 the country's GDP at market prices increased more than fourfold, from 1,319.4 million to 5,281 million Libyan dinars. Oil has become to Libya what phosphates are for Morocco—a major source of foreign exchange.

Politically, Libya's path has diverged from that of its neighbors. Libya owes its liberation to the British Eighth Army, which drove out the Italians in World War II. In 1951 Libya became an independent state based on a loose federation of its three provinces under a monarch. The influx of oil wealth since the early 1960s revolutionized the economy and shattered the social basis on which the monarchy had rested. In 1969 King Idris was overthrown by a military junta led by Colonel Muammar Qaddafi, an ardent admirer of President Nasser, and Libya set out on a path of militant Arab socialism based on the assumption that Qaddafi and his entourage somehow embody the Libyan people.

Qaddafi's economic policy concentrates on industrial development, with major complexes at Misurata and Tobruk. Agriculture has been relatively neglected; the 1976–1980 development plan devoted barely one-sixth of the planned outlay to farming. Libya has established close ties with the Soviet Union, turning Libya into an advanced depot of Soviet weaponry for future use in war. At the same time, Libya has built up a substantial defense force, subsidized terrorist movements in various parts of the world (including the PLO [Palestine Liberation Organization], the IRA [Irish Republican Army], and others), and provided financial and military backing to General Amin, Uganda's former president, to the POLISARIO, and to Muslim separatist movements as far afield as Chad, Thailand, and the Philippines. Libyan agents have made a practice of murdering Libyan exiles abroad in Mafia fashion. In addition, Libya has annexed part of northern Chad (thought to be rich in mineral wealth), and supported plots against President Sadat of Egypt and against General Numeiri, ruler of the Sudan. Qaddafi took the initiative in opposing the Israeli-Egyptian peace talks and has played a major role in setting up the anti-Israeli "steadfastness front" composed of Libya, Syria, Algeria, South Yemen, and the PLO. Qaddafi is trying to extend his sway over Malta, a neutral ministate that commands a great naval base. He also is supposed to be financing efforts to create an "Islamic atomic bomb."

Libya's relations with the United States are peculiar. American corporations such as Exxon, Mobil, Occidental, and others have made substantial profits from their Libyan oil operations, more so than in nearly any other OPEC country, and Libyan administrators openly speak of the benefits that Libya has derived from US technology. On the other hand, Libya today is the most anti-American of all Arab states. As long as Libya's present political course continues, it behooves the United States to oppose Libya with all the means at its command. American interests would be best served by a comprehensive plan of economic warfare, to which Libya's dependence on foreign-imported food makes it vulnerable. The United States might also consider supporting Egyptian expansion at Libya's expense, thereby eliminating a potential Soviet foothold in the Mediterranean and a major center of international terrorism.

ISRAEL AND THE ARAB-ISRAELI DISPUTE

Orthodox Jews believe that they have a covenant with God establishing a kingdom of priests and "a holy nation." The Torah (i.e., the Pentateuch, or first five books of the Bible) is the revealed word of God; ideally, it embodies the constitution of the traditional Jewish polity. A Jew's duty, according to this creed, is to serve God and obey the divinely appointed Law. The Torah may be interpreted according to changing circumstances, but it cannot be changed; traditional Jewish law recognizes neither a separation between church and state nor a division of life into secular and religious spheres.

In ancient times the Torah was the civil as well as the spiritual constitution of the Jewish people, whose leaders were expected to govern according to divine sanctions. After the destruction of the ancient Jewish commonwealth the Jews were driven into exile, but they retained a sense of separate identity. The Torah provided them with a "portable fatherland," while the Law—as interpreted by scholars and sages—gave to orthodox Jews a sense of identity that enabled them to survive the millennia of dispersion ("diaspora") from the Holy Land, from which the Jews, in the believers' view, had been driven out for past transgressions. But the exile, in this view, would not last forever. God, in his own good time, would send a Redeemer to bring salvation to all nations and to lead back the children of Israel to Jerusalem, their holy city.

During the nineteenth century nationalist thinkers began to secularize these religious ideas. The purpose of history was indeed the exiles' return to the Holy Land. But the Jews would be restored through their own exertions, not through the agency of a divinely appointed Redeemer. To this day, a small group of orthodox Jews rejects the state of Israel on the grounds that it, like any other state, is the handiwork of sinful man rather than of God. They be-

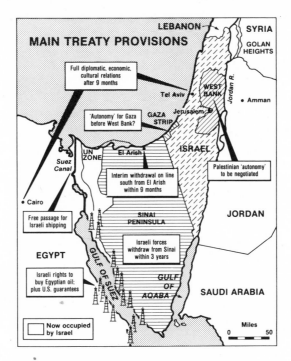

FIGURE 3.2 MAIN TREATY PROVISIONS

lieve that Israel should be redeemed only through a Messiah whose coming they fervently await. But most religious as well as secular Zionists are convinced that the creation of Israel is in some sense linked to a higher purpose, and that its survival is essential for the future of the Jewish people, since it enables them to become a nation instead of a group of homeless wanderers.

Devout Muslims, like devout Jews, also hold that religion is fundamental to human life and destiny. Islam literally means "submission"; the Muslim is one who submits. Man must submit to the word of God as revealed to the Prophet Mohammed and written down in the Qur'an. A separation of life into secular and religious spheres, the notion that religion is man's private affair, is as incomprehensible to traditional Muslims as it is to religious Jews.[1]

Islam divides the world into two great segments: the world of conflict (*dar al-harb*), that is, conflict between believers and infidels, and the world of Islam (*dar al-Islam*) that accepts Islamic law. Through the *jihad* (holy war) the world is to be brought under God's word. Islam needs, then, a political entity to carry out God's will. Arab conquerors imposed Islam by the sword—except on Jews and Christians, who as "scriptural peoples" were given the status of *dhimmis* (tolerated). Though tolerated, they had to accept Islamic rule, pay a poll tax, and endure "humiliations" that at best were symbolic and at worst entailed serious disabilities and even persecution. Modern notions of secular citizenship have today made considerable inroads. But traditional Islam demands that states as well as individuals submit to the will of Allah, and that the tolerated people have limited civil rights.

Islam and Judaism have similarities as well as differences. Both traditionally assume that governments should rule only to carry out God's Law. Both emphasize the Law and offer guidelines for the behavior of individuals and the state. But whereas Judaism demands that only Jews have to accept in full the obligations of the Covenant, Islam insists that the Qur'an was made for all nations and that all "nonscriptural peoples" should be made to accept its tenets. Judaism is not an active missionary religion; Islam seeks to convert the unbeliever. According to Jewish precepts, non-Jews do not suffer civil disabilities but only religious ones. Under Islamic law, nonbelievers have traditionally been subjected to civil discrimination.

The conflict between Arab and Jew, complicated enough in purely secular terms, becomes even more so in religious ones. The Jews argue that they should be allowed to live in the land of Israel, which was given to them by divine dispensation. Most Arabs are willing to let some Jews live in Israel, but they insist that Jews should do so within the confines of a secular state (a solution favored mainly by intellectuals), or of an Islamic state (an ideal that appeals chiefly to the masses). Zionism thus clashes with the political and religious dictates of Islam. Modernization and secularization in Arab and Jewish societies have changed the political vocabulary. Secular-minded Arabs and Jews alike now appeal to natural right and popular self-determination—concepts that have no roots in traditional Judaism or in traditional Islam but that derive from the West. Under the surface, however, religious or semireligious notions remain strong; they profoundly affect Jewish-Arab relations.

But for this religious or quasi-religious component, the conflict might be easier to resolve. In purely material terms, the Jewish "threat" to the Muslim world does not appear great. Israel has taken over a tiny land, insignificant in terms of size or of material resources when compared to the huge territories under Islamic sway. But most Arabs continue fervently to resist Jewish claims. Though wounded Arab pride stands in the way of an Arab-Jewish reconciliation, it is of itself but a minor factor. More important are the demands of Islam, which not only claims sovereignty over the area lost to the Jews but also seeks to Islamize other lands. Hence the Jewish demands for sovereignty clash with the Islamic notions concerning the *dar al-Islam*, with the rights of Israel's Arab inhabitants, and with the issue of sovereignty over Jerusalem, a holy city to Jews, Christians, and Muslims alike. Secular Arab rulers have had little success in defusing this clash of differing religious parties. President Sadat's negotiations in 1979 and 1980 may perhaps best be understood not merely as an essay in realpolitik, but equally as an instrument for the purpose of waging holy war by other than military means; the Israelis, perhaps, may eventually be absorbed into the world of Islam. The growing Arab population within Israel may well encourage such a hope, even though Jewish experience throughout the ages does not support it.

Zionism and the British Mandate in Palestine

The region formerly known as Palestine is now divided between Israel and Jordan; it commands a strategic position at the junction of Asia, Southern Europe, and North Africa. As the Holy Land sacred to Jews, Christians, and Muslims, Palestine has overshadowed in religious importance every other country in the world. Long prey to conquering armies, for four centuries Palestine formed part of the Ottoman Empire. British forces entered Jerusalem in 1917, and five years later the League of Nations placed Palestine—including Transjordan (now known as Jordan), an area east of the Jordan River—under a British mandate.

From start to end of the British occupation, Palestine was a country torn by internal strife. In 1917 the British issued the so-called Balfour Declaration that promised to set up a "national home" for the Jewish people in Palestine. The British offer, made in order to rally to the Allied cause the Jewish communities in both the United States and war-weary Russia, seemed a simple matter of justice to the Zionists—those Jews who looked to the restoration of a Jewish commonwealth in the historic homeland of the Jewish people.

Zionism drew most of its early supporters from the Jewish lower-middle classes and intelligentsia in Eastern Europe, where the Jews mostly spoke Yiddish, a language of mixed origin, mainly derived from medieval German, and enriched by loan words from Hebrew and various Slavic tongues. Most Eastern European working-class Jews held aloof; so did the Jewish upper classes, especially in Western Europe and the United States, who generally sought to be assimilated within the countries of their birth. After World War I, however, the Jewish condition in Europe worsened. Anti-Jewish campaigns in Eastern Europe were followed by the rise of Nazism, and Western humanitarians grew anxious to find a sanctuary for the survivors of Nazi tyranny. To Jewish believers and also to some non-Jewish supporters of Zionism, history makes sense only as an expression of God's will. The Nazi holocaust, then, can be reconciled to the divine purpose only if it can be shown to have contributed in some sense to the restoration of Zion.

In certain respects the Zionist dream succeeded beyond the boldest expectations of its founders. Jewish agricultural colonization in Palestine proved astonishingly successful. Jewish pioneers reclaimed the swampland and irrigated the deserts. The Palestinian economy expanded, and both the Jewish and the

Arab populations increased under the British mandate.[2] No citizen was forcibly dispossessed of his land under British rule. The Zionists, however, never managed to reconcile Arab opposition to their cause. The Jews argued that Palestine should belong to them by right of historic affiliation, by legitimate land purchases, and by virtue of their economic achievements after the purchases, while the Arabs continued to regard Palestine as an Arab country, from which many Palestinians had been unjustly displaced. The savage persecution of Jews in Western countries was, no doubt, regrettable, but hardly a matter of Arab concern; no true believer might countenance the domination of Muslims by non-Muslims.

Jewish and Arab nationalists continued to have a great deal in common. Both shared a distrust of British "imperialism" as well as a pervasive mistrust of Western "materialism," "rootlessness," "urban decadence," and other supposed vices. But Jews and Arabs consistently misinterpreted one another. Zionists, especially the socialists in their ranks, often imagined that Arab opposition to Zionism stemmed only from Arab feudal lords supported by British intrigue; the Arab "masses" were supposedly anxious to cooperate with their Jewish fellow workers against their common oppressors. Arab nationalists, for their part, associated Zionists with the interests of British—and later, of American—imperialists, though Arab theoreticians could not always agree which of their enemies were the puppets and which the masters.

Between these two opposing sides, the British mandatory authorities, never keen in their support of the Balfour Declaration, shifted uneasily. In 1923 the British formally separated Transjordan from Palestine. In 1937 a British commission reported in favor of partitioning residual Palestine into a Jewish and an Arab state, but the project came to nought. The last hope for compromise vanished when the Nazis put into operation their "final solution" for the alleged Jewish "problem." Jews perished by the millions; the very existence of the Jewish people seemed at stake. The trickle of immigrants from Europe became a flood, to which were later added Jewish refugees from Arab countries like Yemen and Iraq. There was bitter unrest and savage fighting. In 1947 the British decided to throw in their hand and the United Nations agreed on a partition plan whereby Palestine was to be divided into a small Jewish and a small Arab state, their boundary lines so complex that only a confederal arrangement could have assured their survival.

Israel: From *Wirtschaftswunder* to Dependence

The Zionists accepted the UN plan. But the Arabs, seriously underestimating their opponents, decided to fight. The Arab armies were crushed; the Jews somewhat extended the boundaries accorded them under the UN partition and would have gained even more territory but for an armistice reached under

UN auspices. The Arabs, however, refused to conclude peace. A state of latent hostility continued between Israel and her neighbors, with guerrilla activities continually flaring up. In 1956 Israel, supported by Great Britain and France, struck at Egypt. Egypt was decisively defeated, but under Russo-American pressure the Anglo-French forces withdrew and Israel was forced to relinquish the Egyptian territory it had seized.

Israel gained a ten-year period of uneasy peace broken intermittently by guerrilla incursions. In 1967 Israel, alarmed by foreign threats and by Egypt's move to close the Gulf of Aqaba to Israeli shipping, struck again. In a lightning campaign the Israelis seized the Sinai Peninsula as well as the Palestinian West Bank, previously under Jordanian control. In 1973, however, Egypt and Syria, well supplied with arms and technicians by the Soviet Union and vastly superior to Israel in numbers, launched a counterattack. Egyptian forces regained control of the Suez Canal, but Syria and later Egypt were again defeated. Egypt was saved only by US pressure and the threat of Soviet intervention. Most of the Sinai, the West Bank, the Gaza Strip, and the Golan Heights remained under Israeli occupation. For the first time in its history, Israel had boundaries that seemed easily defensible; they provided a territorial buffer to guard against surprise attack, and promised military security to a people traumatized by the Holocaust and other forms of persecution.*

Despite Israel's military successes, her diplomatic and economic position continued to deteriorate. During the late 1940s Israel had relied on Czechoslovakia for military supplies; in the 1950s that role was taken over by France. By the late 1960s, however, Israel became solely dependent on the United States for both weapons and diplomatic support. A minor American commitment had turned into an American engagement of enormous financial scope (table 3.2). Diplomatically, Israel had become almost a pariah state, exposed to the hostility of the communist nations, the Arab states, and most Third World countries. Western European countries, once friendly to Israel, increasingly began to side with the Arabs, whose oil wealth gave them a commanding position in the world economy.

Israel's economic dependence on the United States is of recent origin. The first twenty years of Israel saw an economic success story never exceeded in modern history, a Middle Eastern *Wirtschaftswunder* (economic miracle) that rivaled West Germany's. By 1967 Israel was experiencing an economic boom, with a high growth rate facilitated by the steady inflow of foreign capital. The wars of 1967 and 1973 shattered the economy. Israel, itself a tiny country, could maintain its military position only by importing vast quantities of expen-

---

*No nation contains as high a proportion of former concentration-camp inmates as Israel. Menachem Begin, the present prime minister, was himself at one time confined to a Soviet forced labor camp and later recorded his experiences in a classic entitled *White Nights.*

TABLE 3.2
MAIN MIDDLE EASTERN BENEFICIARIES OF US AID 1946–1976
(million $ US)

Country	US Aid
Egypt	
Economic	$2,269.8
Military	. . . . . .
Iran	
Economic	$760.0
Military	$1,412.5
Israel	
Economic	$2,425.6
Military	$5,904.2
Jordan	
Economic	$1,047.7
Military	$551.5

sive military equipment. The result was that government expenditure began to account for an ever-growing part of the GNP. A Jewish story, dating from the 1948 War of Independence, tells of early recruitment to the Israeli navy. The recruitment officer asks a variety of questions: Have you any sea-going experience? Have you served in any foreign navy before? and finally, Can you swim? One of the applicants, standing in line, and having overheard the question, sighs, shrugs his shoulders, and says to his neighbor, "And ships we have not got either!" Those days have long since passed. The Israeli armed forces of today, which depend on a complex technology, would be unrecognizable to the Haganah fighters of the 1940s. By 1979 Israel was carrying the highest military burden per capita of any country in the world. The Begin government's problems were worsened by the country's prevailing political philosophy (Zionist Socialism), which provides for extensive welfare services, extensive government supervision of the economy, and a great array of inefficient public or semipublic enterprises.

As prime minister, Begin hoped to solve the country's economic problems in 1977 by moving Israel away from a planned economy and towards a free market. He removed or reduced currency controls, government export incentives, and domestic food subsidies; he permitted the Israeli pound to "float." These reforms were well intentioned. But by 1979 the country's economic position had once again begun to deteriorate through a combination of high government spending, the high cost of imports, excessive demand for scarce supplies, and some emigration on the part of highly qualified men and women. The system of "linkage," by which taxes, wages, and pensions were adjusted in order to minimize the effects of inflation, in fact further diminished the value of the Israeli currency.

The government experienced great difficulties in forcing Israelis to cut consumption, to confront the powerful labor unions, to improve the productivity of the public sector, and to reduce the power of the bureaucracy. Begin's new economic policy failed to end inflation (which amounted to more than 50 percent per annum by 1979); he failed to expand exports in a substantial fashion or to cut down on government spending. In fact, the government spent even more money than its predecessors; it continued to subsidize unprofitable industries and continued to employ too many unproductive men and women. As a result, Israel became totally dependent on the United States at a time when the Israeli balance-of-payments deficit of $3.25 billion came to equal one-quarter of the GNP, and when the government budget almost equaled the country's output.

The Israeli Dilemma

Israel desperately needs a peace settlement so that it can reduce its military expenditure. If peace should return to the Middle East, foreign investments might return and US aid might be reduced. But even a peace settlement will not solve Israel's problems unless the country learns how to live within its means.

Israel's demographic position is equally unenviable. This tiny country has less than eight thousand square miles, hardly larger than the Principality of Wales and less than one-third the size of Bavaria. Israel has to face the external Arab world; Israel also has a substantial minority problem within her own borders. By 1980, Israel contained about three million Jews and six hundred thousand Arabs; in addition, more than one million Arabs were living on the Israeli-occupied West Bank and the Gaza Strip. Israel's birthrate remains relatively low and Jewish immigration has dwindled to a trickle. The Arabs' rate of natural increase is still high; hence demographers calculate that unless existing trends are reversed Palestinian Arabs will constitute 50 percent of Israel's total population within two decades. If Israel were to insist on retaining the West Bank and the Gaza Strip, the Jews would be a minority within Israel by the end of the century.[3]

From the Zionist perspective, the demographic problem is worsened by the hardening of class lines. The Zionist founding fathers looked to a state in which Jews would do the roughest as well as the most skilled jobs in the economy. For a time they succeeded in their aim. But the Zionists' original objective is increasingly being distorted as labor migrants from the West Bank take over unskilled work from Jews, thus creating a new social problem of the kind that Zionist theoreticians had aimed to avoid. In addition, Israel has to cope with worldwide opposition from displaced Palestinians who live outside the borders of the original Palestine. About 1.5 million Palestinians now live in neighboring Arab states or overseas. In the Islamic world the refugees' position varies sharply. Some are exiles still confined in miserable camps thirty years after the end of the first Arab-Israeli war; others have reached positions of prominence in their new homes and are influential as managers, technicians, and administrators in such countries as Saudi Arabia and Kuwait. But they remain dissatisfied with their conditions—a peril to those Arab governments willing to consider compromise with the Zionists. Palestinians have disrupted Jordan and helped wreck the Lebanon; they still provide a reserve army for militants willing to continue terrorism against Israel and—if necessary—the Western powers.

Politically, they are championed by the Palestine Liberation Organization (PLO), a loose alliance of differing groups, Marxist and non-Marxist. Militarily the PLO does not amount to much. But diplomatically, backed by the Soviet Union and by militant Islamic states like Algeria, Libya, and the new Iran, its position is powerful within the United Nations. The PLO combines terror, propaganda, and diplomacy in a skillful manner; ironically, moderate Arab leaders sometimes are more afraid of the diminutive PLO than of the powerful United States. For the moment, no agreement is possible between the PLO and Israel. Rightly or wrongly, the Palestinians now see themselves as a new nation hardened by the miseries of exile—the "new Jews," driven from their rightful soil by Western invaders. To liberate Palestine requires an "armed struggle"; once Palestine has been freed, "only Jews who were living in Palestine before the Zionist invasion [will] be considered Palestinians."[4]

Israel's position is difficult. Were it to give up the newly conquered regions its frontiers would be hard to defend. If it were to withdraw to the original armistice line, it would have to surrender East Jerusalem; the Holy City would once more be divided. But if Israel were to hold onto the conquered territories it would have to contend with a hostile Arab population, thus endangering its own democratic traditions and alienating American public opinion whose goodwill has become essential to her survival. The Iraqi-Iranian war gave Israel a temporary respite. The Arab front dissolved as Syria aligned with Iran and Jordon sided against Syria. But in the long run, Israel needs peace as much as ever before, lest Herzl's dream of a peaceful, democratic, and independent Jewish state should dissolve into the nightmare of a militarized Jewish ghetto, dependent forever on the United States.

The Sadat Initiative and the Spirit of Camp David

The first sign of a possible breakthrough came with a major shift in Egyptian policy that saw Egyptian president Sadat in Jerusalem to initiate negotiations for peace. Egypt had borne the brunt of the armed confrontation with Israel. By 1978 her economy was in desperate straits; the country needed peace as much as did Israel. In 1978, at the request of President Carter, Sadat met with Israeli prime minister Begin at Camp David. The united Arab front was split; Begin achieved a success that had eluded his predecessors for thirty years. Subsequent negotiations began to falter. As the price for peace, Sadat demanded not only Israel's withdrawal from the Sinai but—for all practical purposes—the creation of an autonomous Palestinian state on the West Bank. At the same time Egypt's existing treaties with the Arab states, it appeared, would continue to take precedence over the peace treaty to be concluded with Israel.

US policy is equally unclear. A minority of Americans consider that the United States made a mistake in backing Israel in the first place, that Israel could not survive without an endless infusion of US money, that America's strategic interests and oil requirements require an alignment with the Arabs, and that Israel should—if necessary—be abandoned.[5] But American public opinion remains overwhelmingly pro-Israeli and strongly anti-Arab.[6] A US abandonment would go against declared American policy as well as contradicting numerous presidential statements. US credibility as an ally would be further shaken in the rest of the world. On the other hand, a substantial number of Americans, including such leading defense experts as Admiral Elmo Zumwalt, prefer all-out support for Israel. They widely sympathize with General Hayim Herzog, Israel's former ambassador to the United Nations, who proposed that Israel should serve as the US military fulcrum in the Middle East. According to Herzog, the cost of US military aid to Israel is a fraction of the $11 billion to $13 billion entailed annually by the upkeep of all US military forces in Western Europe; Haifa, moreover, is a suitable port for the US Sixth Fleet.[7] The Israeli forces form the best and most reliable defense establishment in the Middle East. In any case, they continue, the United States has a moral obligation to defend Israel; the destruction of that nation would be a catastrophe for the West at large.

President Carter took a different line. The president saw himself as a global peacemaker, a role that suits both his domestic political interests and his moralistic convictions. Carter and the State Department originally looked to a comprehensive Middle Eastern settlement in cooperation with the Soviet Union. The Sadat initiative came as a somewhat unwelcome surprise, but subsequently Carter supported it, apparently believing that if Sadat were to fail, he would probably fall from power and US influence would suffer yet another serious blow. The United States, in this view, could not base its Middle Eastern policy on Israel alone; neither could it afford to alienate the entire Muslim world, moderates as well as militants, at a time when the West has grown increasingly dependent on Arab oil. The United States should rely, rather, on moderate Arab states like Egypt and Saudi Arabia and, according to Carter, should persuade Israel—if necessary by threatening to withhold military and economic aid essential for her survival—to make concessions.

The Israelis remain divided. Their troubles have worsened as the Western European states, increasingly dependent on imported Arab oil and disillusioned by the vacillations of United States foreign policy, have begun to sympathize increasingly with the Arab cause. Israel, the hawks argue, cannot afford to make major territorial concessions that would endanger her military security and lead to a second Jewish holocaust. A Palestinian rump state, the third to be created on the soil of the original mandatory Palestine, would come under PLO domination and be a springboard for continued guerrilla attacks on Israel. The hawks are not deterred by world opinion, which they regard as hypocritical. World War II and its aftermath created worldwide refugee problems affecting some thirty million people, yet of all the new nations only Israel is required to make restitution to refugees from its territory. After thirteen years of Israeli occupation, the argument continues, West Bank Arabs enjoy higher living standards, more political freedom, and a greater degree of local self-government than Arabs do in the independent Arab states—certainly than they did during the Jordanian occupation of the West Bank. Since 1967, Arab unemployment has dropped sharply; health services and other social services have improved; Arabs are able to earn substantial wages by working in Israel. Arab newspapermen and Arab municipal councilors are free to criticize the Israeli government, which supports their right to do so even if the more extreme Jewish elements do not. The Palestinians run many municipalities and local administrative bodies; they enjoy already a de facto autonomy. Even if the United States were to guarantee the borders of a diminished Israel, the hawks conclude, such guarantees would not be reliable, given President Carter's proclivity for making rapid policy changes, and given the American record in dealing with allies like South Viet Nam and Taiwan.

Advocates of a compromise peace, on the other hand, argue that the chance of a peace treaty with Egypt might not return; the Camp David agreement, they believe, represents a milestone in the history of Zionism. Continued Israeli occupation of the West Bank, the doves argue, is incompatible with Israel's democratic traditions and endangers its ties with the United States at a time when it has become isolated. Whatever the advantages of Israeli governance, Arabs continue to detest the occupation forces. It would be madness to alienate at the same time the Arab world and the United States, Israel's last remaining ally in an increasingly hostile world.

Towards a durable peace?   From the US standpoint, the best outcome would be a compromise peace reached through a formal agreement between Israel and Egypt. Peace would be costly to the United States but would eventually enable it to reduce military and economic aid to the region and to lessen the enormous tribute it has paid to Middle Eastern governments over the last thirty years. Peace would reduce the danger of confrontation with the Soviet

Union. Peace would slow down the ruinous arms race in the Middle East. Such a peace would best be secured if it were guaranteed not only by the United States but by its Western European allies, especially Britain and France—the very powers spurned so bitterly by the United States during the Suez crisis.

The Israeli-Egyptian peace treaty of 1979 represented an uneasy compromise that did not fully satisfy either side. The treaty entailed a long process of disengagement in which Israel would withdraw in stages from occupied Egyptian territory. Disagreements over the West Bank and Gaza were skillfully masked. Sadat continued to call for Palestinian autonomy on the road to self-determination and statehood, the very objectives that Begin had sworn to oppose. Egypt found herself shunned by the remaining Arab countries, including supposedly moderate states like Saudi Arabia. Syria and Iraq took over the role of Israel's principal enemies. The American taxpayer was asked to shoulder heavy financial obligations in order to give both military and economic support to Israel and Egypt alike. These new commitments were designed to secure a treaty that, by leaving unresolved the Palestinian issue and the future of the West Bank, might contain the seeds of its own undoing.

Nevertheless, the treaty could conceivably turn out to be President Carter's most singular diplomatic triumph. For the first time in its history Israel would have gained formal recognition and acceptance of legitimacy from the most powerful Arab state. A treaty would also serve Egyptian interests. By 1980 Egyptian military planners no longer regarded Israel as their main potential adversary. The Egyptian army had changed the color of its uniforms from desert khaki to jungle green, a switch that, intentionally or unintentionally, symbolized a profound change in strategic thinking. The Egyptians were now mainly concerned with threats from Libya and Ethiopia, both of them Soviet allies. Above all, the Egyptians were determined to keep in power the regime of President Numeiri in the Sudan. Egypt had a vital interest in maintaining a friendly regime in a country that controlled the headwaters of the Nile, Egypt's lifeline. A hostile regime might be in a position to interfere with the regular flow of water, thereby threatening Egypt's very existence. Egypt's army, once largely dependent on the Soviet Union for its supplies, and trained for a mobile desert war against Israel, was accordingly reequipped with Western arms. The Egyptian military provided for quick-strike, airmobile units, capable of ranging as far as the Sudan, Zaire, and perhaps even Somalia.

At the same time, the chances for an Israeli-Egyptian peace settlement seemed better than the most cheerful optimists would have hoped for a year earlier. The unpredictability of the new militant Islamic regime had fostered a climate of apprehension in many parts of the Arab world; to moderate Muslims, Sadat's simple piety seemed infinitely preferable to Khomeini's apocalyptic fanaticism. The guerrilla war in the Western Sahara had diverted attention from the Israeli issue, as had the disputes between such neighboring states as

South and North Yemen, Tunisia and Libya, and Iraq and Iran. Attempts to unite Syria and Iraq had broken down; a Lebanese settlement seemed remote.

Nevertheless, Israeli-Egyptian cooperation still faces many obstacles. A durable peace in the middle East will be hard to make and harder to keep. Americans will have to live with the fact that these are Middle Eastern problems for which no ready solutions are in sight. A Palestinian settlement, however tenuous, requires participation from those Palestinians willing to accept the existence of Israel. It needs extended negotiations with Syria, a country that the United States must woo more effectively than in the past. A settlement would also be strengthened by closer US relations with Saudi Arabia, to which we should offer more effective reassurance.

Planning for Peace

Peace requires sacrifices from both sides. The Arabs will have to learn how to live with Israel just as the Germans have learned how to live without the lands beyond the Oder-Neisse line. Militant Zionists will have to give up their dream of reestablishing the ancient Kingdom of Solomon and of the "ingathering" of all the world's Jewry. Unless the Russians should decide to expel most of their Jewish population or unless there should be an outbreak of anti-Semitism in the Argentine, the sources of Jewish immigration will largely dry up and few Jews will wish to migrate to Israel. As Moshe Dayan regretfully put it, Israel has ceased to be attractive to would-be settlers.

The largest part of the Sinai was never part of Solomon's kingdom or of Mandatory Palestine; the treaty with Egypt was therefore relatively easy to conclude. A long-term settlement of the West Bank dispute will be much harder to reach—perhaps hardest of all. In its own interest, the United States should pressure Begin to give up the occupied territories on the West Bank, the Gaza Strip, and the Golan Heights in return for political guarantees, peace, and US military aid. Special arrangements will have to be worked out for East Jerusalem, arrangements that would prevent the city from being once more partitioned like another Berlin. Should the Palestinians be willing to accept Israel's existence within recognized borders, they should be brought into future negotiations. The Palestinian state will have to be neutralized and demilitarized. Control over the Jordan River will have to be shared by Arab and Jew. The Israelis will have to have forts within the Palestinian state to guard against sudden armored attack on Israel's narrow plains. Not all Palestinian refugees would be able to return to Palestine; but, like world Jewry, diaspora Palestinians would look to the state as their honorary homeland.

The suggested compromise would leave many questions unanswered. There is no way in which the militant members of the PLO can be bought off; they are tough, resolute, and as committed to the absolute justice of their claim as the Zionists. Israel, for its part, will certainly strike back at a West Bank state willing to become an armed sanctuary for guerrilla operations against Israel. For the moment, moreover, the great majority of Arab states are determined to resist the Israeli-Egyptian settlement.

Peace, ironically enough, will bring economic troubles to Israel as well as to Egypt. Israelis will continue to spend a major part of their national income on defense. Life for the Israelis will thus remain hard. The constant threat of war or terrorism keeps people tense. Inflation of 50 to 100 percent a year is a heavy burden, as are the high taxes required to maintain military and large welfare services. An old Israeli joke asks, "How do you make a small fortune in Israel?" The reply: "Come with a large one." Many Israelis have to make ends meet by holding two or three jobs. Until peace is secure, and until the nation can afford to diminish its defense expenditure, Israel will require additional foreign aid.

Assistance from abroad on its own will not, however, solve Israel's problems. Immigration may not revive, but at least the brain drain must end. Perhaps as many as five hundred thousand Israeli citizens now live and work in the United States on a semipermanent basis. The Arab population of Israel and the occupied territories is growing twice as fast as the Jewish population, so the loss of people hurts. The six hundred thousand Arabs who are Israeli citizens, as distinguished from the West Bank and Gaza Strip Arabs, may pose a major threat to Israel in the future. They too are increasing more rapidly than the Jews and may ultimately represent a large part of the population. At the moment the Arabs pose no serious threat to the nation. Most villages are doing quite well and feel relatively content. But as more of their young people are educated in Israeli schools and universities, they will increasingly take part in radical politics. (There were general strikes by Israeli Arabs in 1976.)

At present there is no plan to deal with the future problems of the Israeli Arab. A study should be undertaken to see how they can be integrated into the nation. A policy of peaceful coexistence has to be worked out and the rules of the political game clearly spelled out for Arab citizens; they must know what they can or cannot do. Improvements can be made in Arab housing and education and more opportunities opened to educated Arabs. Until these things are done, the situation will remain explosive.

Egypt's internal situation, unfortunately, is no better than Israel's, though for different reasons. Sadat is popular among the peasants, who supply most of the conscripts and who prefer peace to war. Egyptian industries have made considerable progress; much, too, has been achieved in the agricultural sector. By the end of 1979, Sadat had some genuine economic achievements to his credit. Egyptian oil production had grown. The rate at which savings were being deposited in Egyptian banks had gone up considerably over the previous three years. Industrial exports had gone up over 1978; housing had expanded. Nevertheless, Egypt continues to face a difficult situation. Its population of over forty million produces a GNP smaller than that of Israel ($13.3 billion, as against $14.2 billion in 1977). The Egyptian bureaucracy, like the Israeli, is large, inefficient, and expensive. Over two thousand retired government ministers are on full pay. Most of the economy is backward and cannot quickly be improved, nor can large sums be spent in new aid and loans. Egyptians widely lack management and entrepreneurial skills (the Levantine businessmen who did not lack them were mostly compelled to leave the country during the 1950s). High-cost imported goods are a drain on the economy and there is heavy smuggling to avoid customs duties. The government food subsidy for Egyptians is very high; it is perhaps as costly as the army. An estimated 40 percent of agricultural production is wasted because of an inefficient marketing and storage system. Animals eat most of the wheat, and marketing boards distort the market by paying the highest prices for animal fodder; farmers thus grow clover, not vegetables or fruit. Family planning is badly organized and does not work. The most fertile land, near the Nile, is increasingly being put under roads and houses to accommodate growing demand. Egyptians complain at continued food shortages, high unemployment, wide disparities of income, and endemic graft in Sadat's inner circle.

Egypt, however, shows no sign of weakening. As a nation it lacks both the ethnic diversity and the militant Shi'ite tradition that have contributed so much to Iran's discontent. Nevertheless, Egypt might conceivably have to face in future a combination similar to the one that brought down the shah, namely, a short-lived alliance between the extreme Right (organized in the underground Muslim Brotherhood), dissident army officers, the extreme Left, and organized urban mobs all anxious to smash the regime. The masses do not want war. But the bulk of the intellectuals and professional men do not particularly want peace; they have no wish to cut themselves off from the other Arab countries, many of which provide employment to educated Egyptian emigrants. Arab sanctions against Egypt have worked none too well; by summer 1980 Iraq, Saudi Arabia, and Jordan had all taken up more moderate positions than before, fearful as they were of the revolution in nearby Iran. Nevertheless, Sadat's position is far from enviable. If Egypt is to be kept going, the West may have to help Cairo in overcoming some of its difficulties. This is not a happy prospect for American taxpayers, among whom foreign aid has ceased to be a popular cause as the country faces rising oil prices and a high rate of domestic inflation. Nevertheless, the United States should help for the sake of maintaining the present Egyptian-Israeli compromise. If that compromise lasts for any length of time, peace—however precarious—just may become a habit.

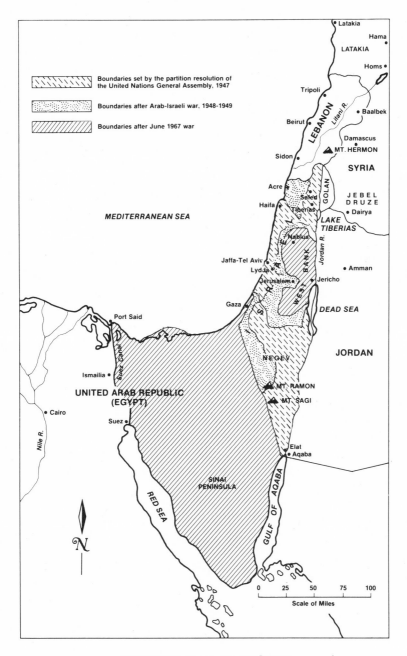

FIGURE 3.3 ISRAEL AND THE LEVANT

LEBANON

Lebanon is a remarkable country. It is a microcosm of East and West with a population that scarcely exceeds 3.3 million. Lebanon's size (thirty-four hundred square miles) is less than one-third that of Belgium. Its natural resources are small; there is neither coal, nor iron, nor oil. Yet hard work by the Lebanese, encouraged by a free-enterprise economy, has turned the country into one of the most prosperous in the Middle East—or had, until civil war broke out in 1975. Lebanon's literacy rate is the highest in the Arab world. The Lebanese have developed a variety of skills needed in secondary industries—banking, insurance, commerce, navigation, and maritime transit traffic—as well as in agriculture, which still accounts for nearly half the country's labor force. In addition, the Lebanese are able, under normal conditions, to make a good deal of money from tourism and from remittances sent home by labor migrants abroad.

Lebanon's troubles are mainly ethnoreligious. The Lebanon, a great natural bastion defended by steep-sided valleys and rocky crags, has traditionally sheltered scores of minority groups. The people are overwhelmingly Arab in speech and cultural affiliation, but Arab traditions have been modified by the impact of the West. French and, to a lesser extent, English are widely spoken in the towns. But there is no true majority. The Lebanese are split between Christians and Muslims, the latter now slightly outnumbering the Christians. Each of these groups is further divided: the Muslims into Sunnis (the largest group), Shi'ites, and Druzes (the last named a semi-Muslim sect); the Christians into Maronite, Greek Orthodox, Armenian, and other churches. The confessional subdivisions are linked to the country's administrative and political system, an arrangement that enables each community to defend itself against its neighbors in a struggle emphasizing communal as much as individual competition. The Muslims are also divided along economic, political, and social lines. The Sunni, generally speaking, are better off than the Shi'ites, who number about 18 percent of the Muslim population, and who have recently acquired increasing importance in the political arena. The Shi'ites have the highest fertility rate among the Muslims, who, in turn, have a higher rate than the Christians. Intermarriage across religious lines is rare even between the different sects within each major faith; hence the chances of demographic unification are practically nil.

The religious split by no means follows class lines; there are many rich Muslims and poor Christians. But in general the Christians were subject to Westernization before the Muslims. The Christians are on the average better educated and hold many of the better jobs. Within the Christian community the Maronites hold the dominant position. The Maronites have traditionally been in communion with Rome. They acquired close links with France and other Western countries; they gained for themselves leading economic, political, and intellectual positions within Lebanon; and they received external support during the period (1920–1944) when the French ran the country under a League of Nations mandate.

Lebanon's so-called communitarian system was confirmed by the National Charter, an informal agreement between leaders of the various communities, especially the Maronites and the Sunnis. This pact assured that the sectarian equilibrium within the country should be reflected in a division of offices at the center, so that the benefits of political patronage, a major economic asset, should not be limited merely to a few confessional groups. The National Charter, however, found numerous critics. As Beirut, the capital city, grew, and as the state bureaucracy became more numerous and more powerful, decentralization of a communitarian kind became ever harder to maintain. The demographic balance of power gradually swung in the Muslims' favor.

According to critics of the Lebanese establishment, the communitarian system entailed the redistribution of spoils from patrons to clients, thereby transforming access to political office into economic power. Economic power in turn rested on Lebanon's service economy, based as it was on trade, banking, and tourism. Employment in the service sector amounted to 55.3 percent of the labor force in 1970; industry provided jobs for only 17.8 percent. Critics found this service economy by itself to be unstable, dependent on booms and busts; it failed to provide adequate employment, discouraged the development of industries, kept Lebanon dependent on the West, and unduly favored Beirut. Mount Lebanon became a kind of residential and economic suburb of Beirut. The less-privileged areas, especially the south and far north, stagnated; rural development programs designed to help them were apt to be shelved.

The Civil War

Conceivably, these difficulties might have been resolved. The Lebanese economy was astonishingly resilient; between 1964 and 1972 alone the industrial sector grew by 115 percent. But Lebanon, politically dependent on an unstable compromise between several communities, was unable to contend with the mass influx of some four hundred thousand Palestinian refugees who gradually formed an armed state within a state. Lebanon's internecine struggles became intimately linked to the wider conflict between Arabs and Israelis—with catastrophic results. Palestinian guerrillas used Lebanon as a base from which to attack Israel. Israeli retaliation drove thousands of refugees from the south to seek safety and jobs in Beirut; the result was unemployment and destitution. The Palestinians had originally resolved to stay out of Lebanon's domestic politics. As factional fighting became more intense, however, the Palestinians failed to maintain their neutrality. They sided with militant Lebanese Muslims of radical persuasion who demanded greater constitutional and economic rights.

In 1975 a bitter and bloody civil war broke out between Christians and Muslims (often misleadingly referred to abroad as "right-wingers" and "left-wingers"). Factional fighting was complicated by private vendettas and gangsterism, both of which spread as more and more arms were slowly and clandestinely distributed among the populace. The Maronite Christians, though traditionally anti-Zionist, gradually drew closer to the Israelis, who supplied them with instructors and weapons. They also raided across the Lebanese border in retaliation for Palestinian guerrilla assaults on Israel from Lebanese bases.

Finally, in 1976, the Syrian army intervened in Lebanon, ostensibly to establish peace between the warring communities, but in fact to tie Lebanon into a greater Syria. The Syrian president and his colleagues were themselves Alawites, members of a minority that did not relish a decisive defeat for the Maronites. Many leftists in the Lebanon also supported the Iraqi branch of the Ba'ath party, an organization with a bitter enmity toward the Syrian branch.

The civil war was a catastrophe for the country. An estimated seventy-five thousand persons were left maimed or dead. Civil war with its attendant atrocities left a legacy of bitter hatred in a land where memories are long and injuries are never forgotten. Worse still were the effects of emigration. Lebanese have always been willing to seek their fortunes abroad. During the civil war emigration intensified; some seven hundred thousand people left the country, of whom only about half decided to return. The emigrants included many of the nation's most skilled and active people—artisans, construction workers, managers, technicians, merchants, and intellectuals. The port of Beirut was paralyzed, the city left in ruins. Most foreign companies established in Lebanon left the country. The physical damage done to the economy was vast. According to the country's foremost experts, the cost of reconstruction alone totaled some $5 billion.

Violence has not disappeared from Lebanon. The civil war may be ended but, as this book went to press in 1980, confessional quarrels as well as gangsterism were continuing and Christians in the south were attempting to run quasi-independent enclaves with Israeli assistance. To complicate the situation even further, the Iranian revolution had induced a new spirit of militance among the formerly quiescent Shi'ites of the south, mostly poverty-stricken farmers who had joined the anti-American chorus.

The New Lebanon and Its Future

Given their troubles, the Lebanese have staged an astonishing economic recovery. Lebanese banking has resumed and extended its operations; the

Beirut Stock Exchange has reopened and once more is a major center of economic activity. Lebanon has resumed its exports; their value in 1978 stood at 1,923 million Lebanese pounds, only 18.5 percent less than in 1977 despite the temporary closure of Beirut's port. Lebanon has found new markets for its products, with Saudi Arabia becoming the country's major customer, while the non-Arab countries have receded in importance (table 3.3).

What of the future? Lebanon is not likely to be absorbed by Syria, which itself faces serious internal troubles. The Syrians have been unable to enforce their will either on the Maronites or on the PLO. Lebanon for all practical purposes is split into several parts, including a divided Christian entity; a rump dominated by Muslim and leftist forces; and a so-called Free Lebanon in the south which, to all intents and purposes, forms an Israeli protectorate under Christian auspices. Syria itself is ruled by a minority of Alawites who, between them, form no more than 11 percent of Syria's population. Alawites predominate in the ruling Ba'ath Party, whose future is uncertain. The party has made a genuine attempt to call for recruits from all sects and all social strata; its members tend to be Arab nationalists; they are not inclined to political fanaticism; the National Democratic Front also provides some jobs to members of other organizations. Nevertheless, Alawite supremacy is by no means stable. Conceivably, Syria might itself break up, with the creation of a secessionist Alawite state centering on Latakia and Tartus. Should this happen, Israel might find herself protected by a cordon sanitaire of Christian, Alawite, and Druze ministates in northern and western Syria and Lebanon, all looking to Jerusalem for protection. The Syrian bureaucracy is competent but the army suffered badly in 1973, and continues to reflect the technical weaknesses and sectarian dissensions that trouble Syrian society as a whole.

Arab support for Syria's position in Lebanon has waned to the point at which Iraq, a member of the so-called Rejection Front denouncing peace with Israel, calls for Lebanese independence. United States interests in this troubled land would best be served by insisting on a neutral Lebanon, independent

TABLE 3.3
DISTRIBUTION OF LEBANESE EXPORTS BY COUNTRY (percent)

Country	1978	1974
Saudi Arabia	36	24
Kuwait	5	4
Iraq	9	5
Syria	9	8
Jordan	11	2
Gulf states	4	5
Other Arab countries	8	6
Non-Arab countries	18	46

SOURCE: *Economiste Arabe* (Beirut) 22, no. 245 (April 1979): 54. Special issue on Lebanon.

of Syria—a country with which Lebanon's ties are relatively limited. This new Lebanon should be built on a federal or a confederal basis that respects the rights of all Lebanese—Shi'ites, Sunnis, Druzes, Maronites, Melkites, Greek Orthodox, Protestants, Armenians—none of whom form a majority. A centralized state cannot be established without another bloodbath. Lebanese neutrality and a measure of internal peace would best be achieved by an arrangement that would at last eliminate militant Palestinians as a military factor while granting effective local autonomy to both the local Christians and the Muslims. This will not be an easy solution to attain, but it is surely the best bargain that can be struck from the standpoint of Lebanese well-being and of American self-interest.

4

Trouble Spots: II.
Iran, the Gulf States,
Saudi Arabia, and Turkey

I ran, the Persian gulf states (including Iraq), Saudi Arabia, and Turkey at first sight have little in common. They are geographically and ethnically diverse; their historical traditions are dissimilar.* Turkish and Farsi, unlike Arabic, do not belong to the Semitic group of languages; though influenced by Arabic culture, each of them has produced a literature quite different from the Arabs'. Iran looks to Afghanistan and Pakistan on the Indian subcontinent; Turkey is a Mediterranean country with links to southeastern Europe as well as to the Middle East. Turkey is relatively industrialized while North Yemen, for instance, lacks a modern manufacturing industry. Turkey depends heavily on oil imports; Saudi Arabia, Iraq, and the Gulf states are among the world's most important exporters of the precious fluid. But all the states within this arc of crisis have one thing in common: they lie within the Soviet line of advance toward the oil wells of the Middle East and toward warm-water ports that might serve the Soviet Union in either the Mediterranean or the Indian Ocean. Their fate, accordingly, will determine the future of the world at large.

IRAN

Iran is a key country in the Middle East. Its physical size is great (six hundred twenty-seven thousand square miles, nearly seven times as big as the United Kingdom); its population is substantial (33.591 million in

---

*Turkey and Iran once ruled great empires and, though beset by foreign threats, never formed part of any Western empire. Iraq and Aden, on the other hand, were once subject to British sway.

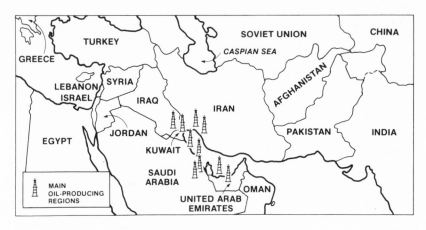

FIGURE 4.1 MAIN OIL-PRODUCING REGIONS

1976). Its natural resources, especially its oil wealth, have made Iran a power with international status. Until recently the economic development of Iran was one of the success stories of the modern world.

Iran under the Shah

Between 1963—the year the shah announced his "White Revolution"—and 1977, the per capita gross national product of Iran went from about $200 to $2,200. There was also a dramatic increase in the gross domestic product, estimated in 1977–1978 at $56,500 million. The rate of petroleum production rose from 1,838.5 million barrels in 1972 to 2,153.0 million barrels in 1976, while manufacturing increased in volume and in kind. New establishments included steel mills, motorcar and diesel engine manufacturers, aluminum smelters, and more traditional enterprises concerned with textiles, food processing, and handicrafts. Iranians saved at an impressive rate. Between 1973 and 1976 national savings reached an annual average of 32 percent of the GNP.

The shah made an effort at land reform. Before 1962, when his program began, about 70 percent of the fertile land had been owned by a small number of powerful magnates. Ten years later, by 1972, more than two million families had benefited from various efforts at redistribution; unfortunately, the shah also took 25 percent of the land for his own use. Cooperative societies were being set up in considerable numbers and subsistence farming was giving way to cash-crop production. During this period Iran had become militarily powerful, its substanital armed forces equipped with the most modern American weapons. Iran seemed to hold the balance of power in the strategically vital Persian Gulf area. The shah cooperated with the CIA, which had helped to put him in power. The shah did everything that development experts on American campuses had advocated: he increased the country's industrial production; he looked to turning Iran from an oil producer to a stronghold of petrochemical industries. The shah protected the Jews; the shah strove for the emancipation of women; the shah opposed the so-called religious reactionaries, and dreamt of a secular state. In the eyes of his domestic supporters and of his foreign friends, Mohammad Reza Pahlavi appeared to be one of the great enlightened monarchs of his age—a new Peter the Great destined to lead his country to modernity.

Why the shah failed   The shah, however, was unable to hold onto power, partly for reasons beyond his control, and partly as a result of his own policy failures. Iran, like many other Middle Eastern countries, had to contend with a runaway rate of urbanization. Students and urban workers, the most volatile part of the population, rapidly grew in numbers. The small shopkeepers were hit by the growth of metropolitan department stores, by inflation, and by ill-considered attempts at price control. Unemployment increased in 1978/79, and despite the expansion of the country's industries—steel mills, petrochemical complexes, even nuclear power installations—the number of applicants for work exceeded the available number of jobs. The shah's White Revolution, entailing land reform planned from above, had alienated the traditional aristocracy without gaining the shah popular support. A large percentage of Iran's landed wealth went to the shah and his protégés. The Iranian smallholders continued to face problems caused by inadequate communications, poor seed stock, lack of modern implements, lack of water, and lack of capital and other such essentials. Land redistribution widely resulted in uneconomic holdings that vitiated the purpose of reform.

The results were revolutionary, but not in the way the shah had intended. Traditional village society grew fragmented; the gap between the haves and the have-nots on the land increased, as did the gap between rural and urban average incomes. Even where the reforms succeeded, farmers continued to face all manner of difficulties. As a result, many villagers left for the cities; for many rural families, farming had ceased to afford an acceptable living. Iranian agriculture became inadequate to feed the country and food imports rose sharply from only $32 million in 1973 to $1.5 billion four years later. The oil boom turned out to be a mixed blessing; the influx of foreign funds contributed to a pervasive inflation that reached more than 30 percent per annum in 1977. The country had to cope with an overblown and underemployed civil service and with a variety of prestige projects of dubious economic value.

In its last years the Pahlavi regime maintained a swollen military establishment; over seven hundred thousand men were in uniform, including regular military units, police, and military gendarmerie. The armed forces, like the great state enterprises, prided themselves on possessing some of the world's most modern equipment. But the striking power of the armed forces, like the productive capabilities of Persian industries, was often diminished by managerial and technological weaknesses. The lower ranks, especially the conscript soldiers, were poorly paid and without social prestige. Iranians of all classes were disgusted at the murders and brutalities of the secret police (SAVAK) and the autocratic nature of imperial rule. Measured against tyrants like Idi Amin or Pol Pot, the shah was not the worst miscreant among his contemporaries—revolutionary propaganda notwithstanding. But he failed to maintain popular support. His Napoleonic ambitions, aimed at making Iran into a great military and industrial power, struck no popular note. His style of governance, his luxury, and his self-isolation turned the masses against him. The great reserve army of students, some of them poorly qualified in a technical sense, looked with apprehension to a future without jobs; urban workers complained that their scanty wages were further diminished by inflation.

Worst of all, the shah did not fully grasp the power of religion in his own country. He shared this fault with his American advisers, with his Iranian supporters, with the leftist intellectuals, and with the liberal opposition made up of educated men and women who perceived the Islamic opposition as a mere expression of political, social, and economic discontent, cloaked in religious language. But the Iranian masses liked the mullahs whose ability to stir up the common people was misperceived alike in Tehran, Moscow, and Washington. The shah's own entourage, the bourgeois opposition, and the Marxists—all equally cut off from their Islamic roots—mistakenly imagined that the shopkeepers and porters in the bazaars, the village cultivators, the hawkers and craftsmen shared the aspirations of well-educated city folk for a secular state and a secularized life. The religious leaders, powerful among the lower-middle class and the poor, were alienated by imperial attempts to control the popular preachers and secularize education, just as they were alienated by the compulsory transfer to private ownership of lands held in trust by Muslim charities: they feared the spread of modernization, especially its religious and cultural consequences. The imperial image became associated with luxury hotels, whores, gambling casinos, and elite department stores. The shah seemed the champion of the smart, the rich, and the foreign; he became hateful to the unemployed and underemployed, to the honest poor, and to the crooks who (as in other nations) continued to play a major part in politics. Moreover, the shah dropped even the pretense of a two-party system. When his position became politically untenable, there was no loyal opposition to take up the reins of government.

US policymakers, however, had little understanding of Iranian realities. The shah's autocratic leanings prevented the development of genuinely supportive institutions, let alone any legal form of dissent. About 1971 cautious support for the shah turned into all-out commitment. US State Department officials, military men, and intelligence officers stationed in Iran learned that no one in the White House wanted to hear anything evil about the shah, who received a blank check to purchase the most modern military equipment on a superabundant scale. The Iranian armed forces were often unable to use their new equipment because of deficiencies in training, maintenance, logistics, and organization. The blank check issued by the Nixon administration continued to be honored by President Carter, though the shah's power was visibly waning. The United States wanted him to act as its policeman in the troubled but important Persian Gulf area and as a powerful ally in the Central Treaty Organization (CENTO), in order to block the Soviet advance into the area.

The Iranian Revolution

The history of the Iranian Revolution remains to be written. The shah vacillated between appeasement and repression, succeeding in neither. His government proved incapable of coping with massive nationwide strikes and the accelerating disorder. The economy faltered as oil production was interrupted. Urban mobs rioted. By January 1979 the army, discouraged and divided within itself, lost control of the streets. Even the middle classes, the main beneficiaries of imperial rule, ceased to back the shah, and the imperial governance collapsed in a welter of disorder and bloodshed. The assault against the shah's regime was accompanied by a skillfully orchestrated propaganda campaign overseas. Iranian student groups, some of them front organizations for the Tudeh Party (an orthodox communist movement unswervingly loyal to Moscow), joined with left-wing intellectuals and radical bodies like the Washington-based Institute for Policy Studies (IPS) to plead the Marxist case. There were three main contenders for power: the army, the Marxists, and the Islamic revolutionaries.

On paper, the army—well armed and numerous—should have won. But having been denied carte blanche to put down the disturbances, it was soon demoralized by a war of attrition. The army also suffered from serious structural weaknesses. The rapid expansion of the armed forces had led to the recruitment of middle-class officers who sympathized with their discontented brethren in civilian dress, and who had little contact with the drafted men from the villages. Rural conscripts proved responsive to the propaganda presented by militant mollahs; they shared the villagers' grievances. There was widespread resentment against American advisers and even more against privileged units like the Rangers (an elite unit) and the Imperial Guards (picked for their loyalty to the monarch). The shah, fearful of army conspiracies, had hermetically sealed the three services from one another; they could communicate only through him, while the chief of staff had been reduced to the position of a quartermaster general concerned mainly with budgetary and logistic problems. Even more unwisely, the shah had insisted that no senior army officer could command units of any corps but his own; hence there was no cohesion even within the upper ranks of the officer class. Had the army been less fragmented it still would have had enormous difficulty in coping with massive strikes in the oil industry and the transportation system. Once the shah—fearful and wavering—had left the country there was no military leader with the will or the personal authority to restore the monarchy. There was a widespread breakdown in discipline, accompanied by interservice rivalry (especially between the army and the air force) and by dissensions between rival political factions. Not surprisingly, the army became paralyzed.[1] Vast quantities of arms fell into the hands of civilian factions. Many conscripts refused to return to duty, preferring to join the Marxist or Islamic militants. For the time being the army could not act against armed civilian formations. But its basic structure, however, remained intact, and its potential power was still considerable.

The largest group contending for power in Iran was that of Islamic revolutionaries headed by Ayatollah Khomeini, an aged religious dignitary. By emphasizing Iran's Islamic legacy, they professed a militant form of anti-Western and religious nationalism that differed from the secular kind proclaimed by Prime Minister Mohammad Mosaddeq two decades earlier.* The Islamic revolutionaries included technocrats as well as mullahs, poor farmers, and members of the urban middle class. These disparate groups were far from united. But they did agree to form a democratic republic and a "new Constitution . . . based on the Islamic Shari'a in the light of contemporary civilization." A comprehensive revolution began that would assure freedom to believers and nonbelievers, a radical change in cultural life, and an end to liquor stores, gambling casinos, and prostitution. The new revolutionary state would not, however, commit the "mistakes" made by the Libyan regime that had adopted nothing but the "superficialities" of Islam. The Islamic revolutionaries were committed to a neutralist foreign policy, aloof both from the United States and the Soviet Union. They condemned the Marxist ideology of the Tudeh Party, but they allied themselves with the PLO, an organization tied in several ways to the pro-Soviet parties of the Middle East and ready to endanger any Islamic government that would refuse to join the struggle against Israel.

On the left, the Islamic revolutionaries faced an array of Marxist bodies. Between them the Marxists were far weaker than their Islamic counterparts;

---

*Mohammad Mosaddeq (Mosadegh), prime minister from 1951 to 1953, tried to build a secular and neutralist Iran. For more than half of his period of office he held dictatorial powers. He nationalized the oil industry, but failed to foresee the consequences of his policy. Oil production faltered; the economy declined; foreign credits ceased to be available; the treasury was emptied. Mosaddeq would have liked to render ineffective or get rid of the shah, but the royalist forces—with Western support—regrouped. In August 1953 they arrested Mosaddeq.

indeed, the Soviet Union appears to have been as surprised as the Western powers by the extraordinary strength of the religious opposition. Nevertheless, the Marxists were far from insignificant. They acquired a following among students, intellectuals, and industrial workers, especially those in the oil industry. The left was divided into a number of armed factions that depended on guerrilla warfare. One of the strongest left-wing groups was the aforementioned Tudeh Party, which was backed by diplomatic, financial, and political aid from the Warsaw Pact countries. The Soviet intelligence services had penetrated the army and SAVAK. Soviet-sponsored publications and radio broadcasts spread "disinformation" designed further to discredit the shah's regime.

The Tudeh Party used cooperation with Moscow and a new alliance with the Islamic revolutionaries as a stepping stone toward a socialist revolution. Negotiations were facilitated through leftist members of the ayatollah's entourage and through Palestinian exiles with a natural interest in a rapprochement between their communist and Islamic supporters. In tune with the current line, the Tudeh Party's first secretary, Iraj Eskanderi, was replaced early in 1979 by Nueddin Kianuri, who vowed to collaborate with Khomeini in setting up an Islamic Revolutionary Council.

From revolution to theocracy   The price of revolution was a heavy one, infinitely greater, it seems, than any of the revolutionaries had anticipated. Iran remained in a precarious position, much worse than in the days of the shah. The economy had been weakened by the large-scale exodus of foreign experts, the failure to maintain or to replace industrial equipment, the extended slowdown of oil production, the effects of continued strikes on banking, business, and industry. Khomeini's attempt to set up a theocratic state aroused bitter hostility among intellectuals, among emancipated middle-class women, and even among Islamic divines of a more liberal persuasion than Khomeini. Militant students who had demonstrated against the shah's regime soon found cause to curse the ayatollah and his lower-middle-class supporters. Worst of all was the uncontrolled seepage of arms into civilian hands. The growth of private armies went with lynch law, kangaroo courts, and administrative disorganization that involved the revolutionary government in serious problems. Iran is made up of many ethnic groups—Persians, Arabs, Azerbaijanis, Kurds, Baluch, and Turkomans. Less than 45 percent of all Iranians speak Persian; the remainder use a variety of other Indo-European, Semitic, and Turkic languages. These minorities owed no loyalty to the new republic, and the breakup of the monarchy—the last of the old multiethnic empires—opened a new era of internal strife as Kurds, Arabs, and other minorities sought concessions from the central government.

In addition, Iran faced a showdown between the religious fundamentalists and the secularists. The leftists included not only the pro-Moscow Tudeh Party, but a new communist party known as the National Communist Party of Iran and a one-time underground guerrilla organization now well armed and experienced in clandestine operations. There were two other Marxist groups. The Mujahedeen e-Khalq (the people's crusaders) were well placed in the universities. The most radical group were the Fedayeen e-Khalq (sacrificers for the people). Working in part underground, the Fedayeen claimed to be Marxist nationalists independent of Moscow. The Fedayeen were also strong in the universities and among the Kurds. Ranged against them were the fundamentalists loyal to Khomeini and the Islamic partisan organization. The moderate republican opposition, whom the United States in its own interest should have consistently backed, found itself in serious straits. Iran now faced the prospect that, after an intervening period of clerical misrule, the Left would take over leadership of all secularists discontented with fundamentalist bigotry, take over the government, and call on the USSR to support the revolution with the Soviet army.

The constitution proclaimed at the end of 1979 was designed to set up what amounted to a clerical state, governed according to the dictates of Islamic justice. Khomeini became supreme spiritual leader; he was endowed with vast and ill-defined powers to reform the nation and to command the armed forces. The army was committed, not merely to the defense of Iran's borders, but also to waging a holy war for the purpose of expanding God's Law in the world and striking terror into the hearts of infidels. The spiritual leader appointed the chief justice, as well as experts in Islamic law who sat on a Guardian Council designed to ensure compliance with the Qur'an for all laws passed by the National Assembly. The secular element was represented by an elected president; much would depend on his ability to run the ship of state in the face of clerical interference.

Liberty fared badly under the new constitution—worse, even, than under the shah. The victims of the new regime included not merely royalists, but political dissidents within the revolutionary ranks, members of ethnic minorities, religious offenders, homosexuals, and prostitutes, as well as ordinary men and women who had the misfortune of being denounced by their neighbors over some local quarrel. SAVAK, the shah's secret police, was reconstituted under the new name of SAVAMA, but its methods changed little. Whereas the shah had alienated his neighbors, especially Iraq and Saudi Arabia, by initiating an arms race in the Persian Gulf, the ayatollah made foreign enemies for himself by revolutionary propaganda among Shi'ites living beyond his country's borders. Secular megalomania gave way to religious megalomania, with disastrous effects.

The Muslim militants in Iran profess to restore the purities of traditional Islam. They look to the past, to an era in which gambling casinos and "pornographic" movies were unknown. But traditional Islam did not manipulate the news media, as does Khomeini with so much skill, nor did it glorify the revolution of the masses. Perhaps most important of all, traditional Islam had no sense of inferiority with regard to other civilizations—quite the contrary. Today's militants are nearer in spirit to the clerico-fascists of Eastern Europe two generations ago than to the Islamic thinkers of old; they hate the United States because they equate it with ungodly wealth, materialism, moral permissiveness, and all-round metropolitan degeneracy. Like the adherents of the romantic creeds on which European fascism was based, they love to contrast the supposed profundities of the "folk soul" with their enemy's "shallow rationalism." Dissidents like the Bahai paid with their lives.

The anti-American gambit   Anti-Americanism also provides the Iranian leadership with tactical advantages. The seizure of the American embassy at the end of 1979 diverted popular attention from a variety of ills. Iran was internationally isolated, fearful of Soviet designs, and apprehensive of Iraqi ambitions to become the leading power in the Persian Gulf and to support Iran's Arab minority. At home, Iran had to contend with the problems already described. The takeover of the embassy, in contrast, intimidated pro-Western elements in Iran while striking a symbolic blow at the shah's main foreign protector, the principal capitalist power, and the supposed "Satan." For a time, the assault united militant Muslims and militant leftists in a common enterprise that, briefly, muted their mutual hostilities. Above all, the move against the embassy—cleverly stage managed, and publicized all over the world by news-hungry Western television media—provided an agreeable spectacle to the many discontented Iranians whose economic position had become worse than it had ever been under the shah.

There is no denying that Ayatollah Khomeini's appeal among Farsi-speaking Iranians has been considerable. For instance, the ayatollah—at the time of the elections—enjoyed great popularity among small Muslim farmers in the backwoods and the urban poor in the bazaars. Tenants loyal to the revolution took over the former landlords' estates and ceased paying rent. The government attempted to make credit facilities available to peasants who had never before enjoyed such advantages. The revolutionaries respected the countrymen's customs; boys and girls were separated in the classrooms of village schools; women were enjoined to observe a modest demeanor and wear the traditional chador, a black veil. Traditional values were publicly vindicated: Islam stood supreme. The foreigner at last had been shown his place!

Iran falls apart   Unfortunately, however, the revolutionaries failed to set up a new order. There was no equivalent to Cromwell's New Model Army, to the clubs of Jacobins that helped to organize the revolutionary regime in France, or to Lenin's Communist Party at the time of the October Revolution. The mob took over in the capital; the clergy—dependent as they were on popular support—failed to oppose mob rule. The existing administration broke up, to be replaced by a plethora of vengeful revolutionary committees and kangaroo courts. The army, though not a neglegible force, was in no position to unify the country, or deal effectively with discontented minorities. For the time being, the country's only unifying ideology was anti-Americanism. Meanwhile the surviving adherents of the shah believed, apparently with much justification, that American pressure had prevented the army from seizing power while there was still time. Only the future would show whether Khomeini would turn out to be the Kerensky rather than the Cromwell of the Iranian Revolution.

Under these circumstances, the choices open to the United States were limited. President Carter placed an embargo on Iranian oil imports, froze Iranian funds in US banks, and began to consider other forms of economic and military sanctions. By these actions he regained some of his lost popularity. For the first time since the Vietnam War, there was a resurgence of American national sentiment; much to the Iranians' surprise, the campus crowds and the television commentators did not rally behind the ayatollah; American pacifism had sustained a heavy loss. Instead of downplaying the hostage issue, Carter unwisely approved a commando-style action to rescue the hostages; the attempt failed, thereby strengthening the Iranians' position. Iranian students and residents in the US suffered some harassment. Their protests occasionally made unpleasant reading to those Americans aware of the kind of treatment that Iranians would have meted out to Americans in Iran had Americans seized Iranians in the United States. Direct military action, however, did not seem a remedy, except for injured pride; there was, for instance, no point in disrupting Iranian oil production through a military assault, however successful.

The victory attained by Abolhassan Bani-Sadr in Iran's first presidential election early in 1980 seemed a hopeful sign. Bani-Sadr, a supposed moderate with a Western education, mustered substantial popular support. By summer 1980, however, there seemed no indication that the new president would be able to rebuild the country's shattered administration, reorganize the army, and restore national unity. At the same time, the Iranian government faced a multitude of perils. The US boycott, imposed in retaliation for the seizure of the American hostages, entailed serious economic problems. Much more dangerous was the threat from Iraq, which was disputing not only the Iranian borderlands and Iran's possession of several strategic islands in the Persian Gulf but its former primacy in the area. Faced with an Iraqi attack, the Iranians defended their country with resolution unexpected by their enemies. The minorities failed to take up arms on behalf of the Iraqi invaders. The arms supplied in the past by the United States turned out to be an unacknowledged blessing. War in fact may have helped to consolidate the revolution. But Iran's long-term economic and political problems remained to plague the country.

In the long run, the Iranian government is in danger of being gradually subverted by a coalition of left-wingers and ethnic dissidents who might later call for Soviet armed aid. If the Soviets were to invade, the Iranians would certainly wage guerilla war. But the Tehran authorities are in no position to resist a Soviet invasion. The Soviet occupation of Afghanistan has outflanked Iran strategically; Soviet airpower has been brought closer to the Strait of Hormuz. After many years of neglecting its military forces, the United States is in no position to intervene militarily for the purpose of defending Iran. Morally, the Soviet success in Afghanistan has weakened the Soviets' diplomatic position within the Islamic world. But the effective deployment of Soviet power has also given new arguments to those who consider that the Soviet Union is too strong to be resisted. The Soviets have understood only too well the truth of Al Capone's aphorism that more is gained by kind words and a gun than by kind words alone.

Options for US Policy

Unless it repairs its weaknesses, the United States might have to consider an old-fashioned "spheres-of-influence" agreement with the Soviet Union. This would recognize that Afghanistan and Iran lie within the Soviet sphere of influence, and that Saudi Arabia and the remaining gulf states lie within the Western sphere. Given the importance of Iran's oil to the Western world, such an arrangement would be a bitter pill for the West to swallow; it would also be difficult to enforce, unless the United States can convince its allies that it is willing to engage in a serious long-term rearmament program, that its policy will not suddenly twist and turn, that it is resolved to defend what remains of its stake. The United States will have to improve its relations with Turkey, a subject to which we shall return. It will have to preposition troops and military supplies in the Sinai Peninsula, for ready use in the gulf area. It will have to be ready to move into Saudi Arabia, should the Soviets occupy Iran. It will not be able to do any of these things unless it succeeds in greatly strengthening its conventional military forces, recreating military units skilled in special operations, and making arrangements in advance to supply partisans with automatic weapons, ground-to-ground and ground-to-air missiles—weapons of the kind that the Soviet Union and its allies routinely supply to "liberation movements" all over the world.

In addition, the US administration must learn how to discipline its members to speak with one voice rather than in a discordant chorus. The president and his advisers must resist the temptation to act as arbiters of the world's conscience, to comment in public on the real or supposed moral shortcomings of our actual or potential allies—a practice that has contributed so much to the deterioration of our strategic position throughout the world. The United States has to reorganize its intelligence operations, giving personal responsibility for the quality of local reporting to the ambassador accredited to each foreign government rather than to some impersonal "country team." American military thinking should place more emphasis on leadership and morale and less on the managerial approach; Americans must once more learn the lesson that wars are won by men in battle, not by systems of analysis.

Even more important, American public opinion has to be persuaded just how perilous the situation has become. The greatest strategic revolution since World War II has taken place without any public understanding of its nature. Twenty years ago, the Western position in the Middle East and Western access to Middle East oil were reasonably secure. Today, the Soviet Union threatens to take the West's place. The Soviets' military strength, their airlift capacity, and their political influence have grown apace. The United States has seriously declined in all three, at a time when both its and its allies' dependence on imported oil have vastly increased.

The United States must also learn how to accept the Soviet Union's ideological challenge—not an easy task in the absence of "American" parties corresponding to the worldwide network of pro-Soviet communist parties. Americans nevertheless enjoy potential advantages. The Tudeh Party's association with the Soviet Union might be turned into a weakness if it were made a reminder of the USSR's past territorial claims on Iran. A Shi'ite revolution backed by left-wingers is bound to arouse fears in Iraq, where a Sunni minority continues to exercise its sway over a Shi'ite majority. Americans would also do well to point out the close association of communism with a "new class" of party functionaries and ideologues—an exploitative stratum accustomed to use Marxism-Leninism itself as a class ideology. We should also publicize the sorry record of all Marxist radical regimes who, having reached power, have suppressed civil liberties, attacked religion, and betrayed every decent ideal.

We Americans also need to respect the force of religion in politics, especially in Islamic countries such as Iran. We shut our eyes to SAVAK, to corruption and inefficiency, and to the haste in which the shah tried to modernize a feudal society. In so doing he alienated students, the middle class, the workers, and the religious leaders. We should have foreseen the dangers of his one-man rule, his too rapid pace of change. We should have restrained our sales of advanced weaponry and of industrial equipment—sales that required the presence of forty thousand Americans in a land traditionally sensitive to foreign domination. We are in danger of making the same mistakes in such other parts of the Middle East as Saudi Arabia and Egypt.

American propaganda should draw attention to the nature of Soviet rule over the Muslims of Central Asia and to Russia's past attempts to expand its territory at the expense of Turkey and Iran. We should belabor the official atheism proclaimed by the Soviet regime, the disabilities imposed on adherents of Islam in the Soviet Union, and the Soviet record of religious oppression. Such language would appeal to the mullahs as well as to mass audiences. With this change of strategy, the United States would have a chance not only to repel the Soviet ideological offensive but even to carry the war of words into the Soviet Union itself, where Islamic revivalism is a potential force among the vast and growing Muslim minorities.

Above all, United States policy makers should stress again and again that the values of the American campus are not necessarily those of America at large, that America is not the enemy of all traditional values, and that we hold religion and the family in respect. The conservative reaction is a worldwide phenomenon. The time has come for us to profit from its impact.

THE PERSIAN GULF STATES

We cannot quickly reduce our dependence on oil from the Persian Gulf, and we shall have to protect our supplies there while we search for alternate sources of oil and new modes of energy poduction. Few areas in the world are as vital to Western Europe and the United States as the Persian Gulf states (which for present purposes exclude Saudi Arabia). By 1979, the United States was obtaining more than 25 percent, Western Europe about 50 percent, and Japan something like 70 percent of its oil from the Persian Gulf. This percentage continues to increase at a time when the Western position in the Middle East has much diminished both in the military and the political sense. If published CIA predictions are correct, the world's demand for oil will substantially exceed the world's producing capacity by 1983. Saudi Arabia will continue to occupy a key position until 1983; thereafter the gulf states may well become America's principal foreign source of supply.

The transformation of the Persian Gulf states is relatively recent. After World War II the gulf area became one of the world's principal sources of

TABLE 4.1
ESTIMATED DEMAND FOR MIDDLE EASTERN OIL
(in millions of barrels per day)

Year	United States	Europe	Japan
1973	3.30	12.80	4.20
1980	14.00	19.00	9.00
1985	18.00	24.00	12.00

SOURCE: Patrick Wall, ed., *The Indian Ocean and the Threat to the West* (London: Stacey International, 1975), p. 184.

petroleum, an "oil revolution" that occasioned a profound social and economic upheaval and had far-reaching political consequences. The oil states were drawn one by one into the wider circle of Arab politics during the 1960s and, after 1967, into the Arab-Israeli dispute and the orbit of great-power diplomacy. Great Britain was the traditional ruling power in the region. The British had maintained peace and a local power equilibrium through special treaty relations with Kuwait, Bahrain, Qatar, the Trucial States (a group of sheikhdoms so named because of the "truces," or special treaties) and Oman. During the aftermath of World War II, however, British power rapidly declined and in 1971 Great Britain withdrew from the gulf. Although Britain could no longer shape events in the area, the United States hesitated to step in to fill the vacuum. By a strange and perilous quirk of fate, the economic well-being of the United States and its leading allies has come to depend on a congeries of small, weak, backward, and bitterly divided states whose political future remains in doubt.

On the local level, the Persian Gulf states have to contend with the ambitions of Saudi Arabia, Iran, and especially Iraq, all of them bigger fish than the local sheikhdoms. Most important, the region has become an object of Soviet ambition, which the gulf sheikhdoms, some of them strange medieval survivals, are in no position to resist on their own. The sheikhdoms are also threatened by internal subversion, by their own instability, and by their petty dissensions; in the future they may also have to face the intervention of Soviet proxy forces (Cuban or perhaps East German). The menace to Western security is indeed considerable.

The Strait of Hormuz is the strategic key to the area. By mid-1977 about 60 percent of the noncommunist world's international waterborne oil traffic passed daily through this strait aboard some forty-two tankers. Throughout the gulf these ships are vulnerable to precision-guided missiles from the shore; their vulnerability increases while they are navigating the narrow channel along the southern shore.

Oil and the New Proletariat

Though the Persian Gulf oil states differ among themselves in many ways, they have certain features in common. Their populations are small; Kuwait, the most prosperous of the group, has just over a million people, the United Arab Emirates less than a million, Qatar about two hundred thousand. Their gross national products, however, are vast; Kuwait's in 1975 was $13.9 billion, the United Arab Emirates, $4 billion. The gulf states have few resources other than oil, which dominates the local economy throughout the region. They are beset by incredible contrasts between poverty and affluence. Their wealth depends on immigrants, who do most of the productive work. Native Kuwaitis,

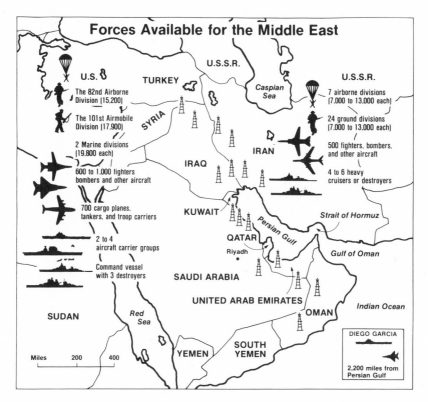

FIGURE 4.2 FORCES AVAILABLE FOR THE MIDDLE EAST

for instance, make up only about 40 percent of Kuwait's population; the remaining 60 percent are immigrants of other than Kuwaiti nationality. These newcomers include two hundred and seventy thousand Palestinians, Indians, Pakistanis, Arabs from neighboring countries, and other nationalities. Kuwaitis provide only about 20 percent of the labor force, yet more than 70 percent of them are on the government payroll. The proportion of indigenous people in Abu Dhabi is even less, perhaps one-third. Indigenous Arabs predominate only in Bahrain and Oman, but even these countries have large foreign minorities.

The immigrants often perform most of the tasks that natives cannot or will not perform, but the immigrants' rewards sometimes bear little relation to the value of their work.[2] The rulers of Kuwait, Qatar, Abu Dhabi, Oman, and Dubai have devoted a considerable proportion of their oil revenue to providing subsidized or free housing, schooling, medical services, cash grants, and jobs for their subjects. These benefits have been confined mainly to the indigenous people, who receive special advantages in employment. Such practices have resulted in an elaborate system of financial privileges for the locals and in discrimination in employment for the immigrants that goes far beyond anything found, for example, in South Africa. Indigenous citizens receive jobs even though they may be barely literate; in consequence, they become privileged state pensioners while disqualified foreigners do the real work. There is similar discrimination with regard to civil rights. The rulers of most gulf states, especially Kuwait, place obstacles in the way of obtaining local nationality and citizenship, causing the immigrants to harbor feelings of bitter resentment toward the governments and the subjects of the countries to whose prosperity they have contributed so greatly. Whatever differences may divide them, many Palestinians, Egyptians, Iraqis, Syrians—the "northern Arabs"— are united in their resentment of the gulf Arabs and in their feelings of superiority to them.

Destabilizing Forces

Not surprisingly, the gulf states, except for Kuwait and Bahrain, are unstable. Bahrain is in a relatively healthy condition, for in addition to the sale of its oil it gains a substantial revenue from its role as a trading depot and purveyor of mercantile and banking services. Bahrain is planning to become the commercial service and support center for the Persian Gulf. Bahrainis have established an aluminum industry and a ship repair yard. (A road to link Bahrain to Saudi Arabia is scheduled to open in 1983.) The proportion of foreigners in Bahrain is less than 20 percent, and Bahrainis are relatively well educated. Oman lies at the opposite end of the spectrum. The reigning sultan has ambitious plans for improving his people's condition; but the great majority of Omanis have as yet been little affected by the discovery of oil in their country. They remain illiterate, ravaged by endemic diseases and suspicious of outsiders and their innovations. A large proportion of the wealth derived from Oman's oil is devoted to armaments.

The future of the gulf states looks uncertain. The people are divided by tribes into warring factions and the immigrant communities are not likely to long endure their situation. The development of the oil industry is helping to create a new, discontented proletariat; hence internal unrest will certainly increase. The gulf states have also to contend with the ambitions of the adjacent Islamic states—Iran, Iraq, and Saudi Arabia. The Iranian Revolution has made the situation even more tense than before. According to the Shi'ite militants in Iran, the Islamic Revolution knows no boundaries; Kuwait and Bahrein, then, should both become "Islamic states." Iraq with its Sunni ruling class and Shi'ite majority, naturally feels threatened; the Iraqi regime, whose armed forces are somewhat superior to Iran's, have promised to intervene on behalf of Kuwait and Bahrein. Iraq has also lent support to Arab separatists in Iran's oil-rich province of Khuzistan (known to Iraqis as Arabistan). In September 1980, open war broke out between Iraq and Iran at a time when Iran's armed forces seemed in disarray and Iraq's army had been reequipped by the Soviet Union. The consequences for the West were likely to be serious. Ongoing hostilities were likely to strengthen the position of the Soviet Union. The world's oil supplies might well diminish, with particularly severe consequences for poorer countries like Turkey. Iran became even more isolated within the Arab world than it had been before.

The future is hard to fathom. Ironically, the ayatollah's regime has turned the United States into an enemy at a time when Iran needs every ally it can get. The ayatollah, however, cannot easily diverge from his radical path without abandoning power. His support for the PLO threatens further to destabilize the Persian Gulf and Saudi Arabia. Khomeini activists are at work among the Shi'ites of the gulf, their religious study groups can be turned into potential fifth columns. The Shi'ites at present work in informal collaboration with the Palestinians that form a considerable proportion of the population in Kuwait (20 percent), Qatar (22 percent), the United Arab Republic (30 percent), and elsewhere in the gulf region. More than a hundred thousand Palestinians work in Saudi Arabia, where they hold important jobs in the oil industry and even in the army. These gulf Palestinians are by no means united. The most radical group is the militant Popular Front for the Liberation of Palestine, led by George Habbash, which works secretly among them. Palestinians also live on the Iranian side of the Persian Gulf. They form a potential threat to all local states. Hence the West has to reckon with a new Shi'a-Palestinian alliance that could become capable of drawing on Soviet aid in order to destroy oil fields, block the Strait of Hormuz, or even take over the smaller states in the area.[3]

The Soviet presence   According to reports in 1979, the Soviet Union has built massive military installations in South Yemen. The Russians have large military supply depots there, depots that will make airlifts unnecessary in the event of war. In addition, the Soviet Union is reportedly training a large airborne strike force made up of Palestinians, South Yemenis, and Ethiopians; this force, supposedly forty thousand men strong, will be supplemented by a corresponding paratrooper force in Ethiopia called the Proletarian African Division. According to reports in *Die Welt* and the *New York Times*, in the event of war this force could be airlifted to the Persian Gulf in order to seize the oil wells and forestall Western intervention. The Soviet Union's bargaining position has been further strengthened through its close contacts with the PLO.

The Soviets reinforced their new position in the Middle East when, in December 1979, they launched an invasion into Afghanistan in support of a satellite regime. The Soviet move had far-reaching consequences. For the first time since World War II the Red Army, not proxy troops, massively participated in the occupation of a neighboring country outside Eastern Europe. The invasion gave proof of thorough military coordination between the various Warsaw Pact countries. The Muslim states of the Middle East received notice that, given the apparent weakness and lack of resolution displayed by the Western powers, they had better collaborate with the USSR, or suffer the consequences. Pakistan was directly threatened; Iran was strategically outflanked; a Soviet invasion of Iran at some future date in support of a left-wing "liberation movement" seemed a possible danger. In addition, the Soviets gained access to Afghan air bases at Kandahar, Shindand, and elsewhere, with far-reaching military consequences. Soviet combat aircraft and troop transport planes were now within less than three hundred miles' range of the Strait of Hormuz. They were also within easy striking distance of targets in Iran and of the US naval forces in the Indian Ocean. Hence Soviet aviators, tactical or long-range, no longer were under the necessity of flying the thousand miles or so from the Soviet bases in South Yemen or of overflying Iran and Pakistan in order to strike at American forces or Western tankers in the Indian Ocean.

What the West Can Do

In 1979 Oman asked the United States for arms and training facilities. The United States responded favorably, and wisely so. Omani bases dominate the Strait of Hormuz, the spigot, so to speak, that provides passage for much of the world's oil traffic. The two countries reached a basic agreement whereby the US Air Force will gain access to three important Omani air bases, while the US navy will obtain access to Omani ports. In return, the United States will pay for improvements to these bases, supply the Omani armed forces with new weaponry, and defend the Kansas-sized sultanate in the event of a Soviet attack. At the same time, the United States took steps to gain facilities in Kenya and Somalia. The Omani bases, however, are much nearer to the Strait of Hormuz than either the equivalent facilities in Kenya and Somalia or the existing Western base on the remote Indian Ocean island of Diego Garcia. Saudi Arabia is threatened by the militant Shi'ite minority and by the alliance between Khomeini and the PLO, a point to which we shall return. In addition, the United States has sent military aid to North Yemen. But military hardware alone will not suffice. US policy in the area as a whole should be directed toward the gradual emancipation—through promoting civil rights, equal pay, and social services—of at least the skilled immigrant communities; an ever-present irritant would thus be removed. The United States should resist the attempts of either Iran or Iraq to establish a hegemony; instead it should seek to preserve the status quo, which is most conducive to American interests. This will require the ability to deploy naval and military power in the gulf in order to deal with potential threats. The Soviet Union and Cuba should be left in no doubt that the security of the gulf is of vital interest to the United States and its western allies, and that the United States will not tolerate armed intervention through Cuban or other Soviet proxy forces.

The control of Persian Gulf oil and the gulf itself are great prizes to either side, and the political instability of the area offers many opportunities for subversion and conflict. Unfortunately, the gulf cannot be neutralized at this time; Iran can no longer act as its policeman, and Iraq is an undesirable successor to that role. The greatest barrier to keeping the status quo is the USSR, which is supporting the so-called liberation groups and encouraging the advance, for example, of South Yemen into North Yemen and Oman. This drive must be thwarted if peace and stability are to endure.

No Western power is ready to establish a protectorate in the gulf; maintenance of the status quo thus seems to be the best policy for the moment. But if instability continues and Marxist takeovers threaten to capture the West's oil supply, the United States must be prepared to intervene and also forge mutual security pacts with local Arab governments. Meanwhile it can try to shore up the existing governments, direct the training of their military and police forces, send technicians and engineers to guide their development, and warn the Soviets to leave the area alone. The Arabs should be cautiously encouraged to form an alliance system that will preserve the present governments in power and defend them if necessary with men and material. The form of this security system can be loosely structured, but it needs a formal organization that can act quickly to stop war or revolution. A coalition of Arab states was able to stop the threatened invasion of North Yemen in 1979, but something more structured is needed. By the use of careful diplomacy the United States might contribute to an effective alliance system to protect the area. We Americans have to show resolve; like OPEC, we should form consumer cartels and use the bargaining strength of our technical prowess, industrial goods, and food. Then, if all our efforts fail to guarantee uninterrupted supplies of oil, we and our allies should intervene. We should profit from South Africa's experience and build up, as the South Africans have done, a substantial strategic oil reserve—no matter whether the Saudis object or not. We should encourage conservation at home. Above all, we should offer the domestic oil industry lower taxes in exchange for greater savings and investment. Instead of taxing the industry, we should tax imported oil, while giving exemptions to countries like Canada, Mexico, and Venezuela that are likely to remain secure sources of supply.

As we have already pointed out in our section on Iran, we may, for lack of an effective policy, be forced to envisage Soviet control of Iran in the not-so-distant future. The defense of the smaller gulf states and of Saudi Arabia therefore becomes even more important for the sake of our survival and the survival of our Western and Japanese allies. The point bears repeating that additional military preparations must be made. The Soviets already have a force trained to intervene in the Persian Gulf; they have an impressive airlift capacity; they can overfly Turkey and Iran with impunity; they have the advantage of proximity, whereas our own bases at present are remote. The Joint Chiefs of Staff now wish to build up a Fifth Fleet in the Indian Ocean, where the Soviets already maintain a substantial force. A large and well-equipped US strike force is being developed to assist oil-producing states threatened by rebellion or invasion, or to seize selected oil fields.

On the diplomatic front, it behooves the United States to oppose the new radicalism represented by the PLO-Iranian alliance. We should work to counter it by cooperating with Saudi Arabia and the gulf states. This will be possible only if the Israel-Egypt treaty produces good results, and the PLO will have to participate in all peace negotiations to make them effective. Meanwhile we should build up a mobile, heavily equipped strike force of thirty thousand or forty thousand men ready for desert warfare and able to block Soviet takeovers or those of their radical allies. Material and equipment can be prepositioned in the Sinai bases abandoned by the Israelis. Bases in the Sinai, manned by Egyptian and US troops, are likely to be more effective than a rapid-deployment force from Europe or the United States. Egyptian forces should be upgraded in training and equipment so that they can protect the West's oil supplies in times of emergency. Other Arab states should be assisted with training and equipment to ensure their security. Above all, we should cooperate more closely with our West European allies; in case of need, we should not hesitate to draw on assistance from Pakistan.

SAUDI ARABIA

Saudi Arabia is a huge country: its almost nine hundred thousand square miles extend over four-fifths of the Arabian Peninsula. Most of the country is wasteland or desert; only a tiny proportion has arable, cultivated, or pasture lands. Saudi Arabia is the greatest oil producer in the Middle East, commanding about 33 percent of available oil capacity in the Middle East and nearly 40 percent of its oil reserves. Although its principal wealth comes from oil, farming still remains the country's main occupation.

Before the exploitation of oil Saudi Arabia depended largely on simple exchange between nomads who raised livestock and farmers who produced food. Its largest single source of income came from tourists and pilgrims to the holy cities of Islam. The oil resources were largely developed by Aramco (Arabian-American Oil Company), a huge American company that built up the oil industry, and its extensive ancillary services, to a level involving an immense transfer of capital and industrial expertise to the Middle East. During the 1970s the Saudi Arabian government acquired an increasing share in the company's ownership; in 1977 it started the process of taking over complete control. Aramco continues to run the industry, however, and has revolutionized the Saudi Arabian economy.

The oil company has paid most of the country's taxes, part of which has been invested in improved communications, schools, hospitals, irrigation works, desalinization programs, petrochemical plants, and similar enterprises. Saudi Arabia's Second Development Program, announced in 1974, called for an expenditure of about $140 billion between 1975 and 1980 compared to only $12 billion between 1970 and 1975. Villages have grown into cities; airfields, roads, and port facilities have been constructed or expanded. A complete welfare program is now in operation; it offers free medical care and schooling to most Saudi citizens. The country has become a major source of contracts for foreign firms—especially US ones, which in 1976 alone received contracts worth over $27 billion. Revenue derived from the oil industry has provided Saudi Arabia with a vast amount of liquid capital capable of being invested abroad; once again, US partners are preferred. From being one of the world's most backward countries, Saudi Arabia has become a great financial power able to give much-needed financial help to states like Egypt that, intrinsically, are more powerful than Saudi Arabia.

Problems of Development

Rapid development, however, has also had the effect of creating tremendous social imbalances, so that in some respects Saudi Arabia resembles prerevolutionary Iran. Admittedly, the parallels are not exact. Saudi Arabia does not have problems with its minorities comparable to Iran's with the Kurds, although there are tribal divisions; most of its population speak Arabic and nearly all practice the Islamic religion. The rulers have followed a puritanical form of Islam, thereby avoiding hostility from traditional Muslims anxious to defend their faith against the alleged iniquities of the West. Nevertheless, Saudi Arabia has its troubles. While Iraq, with a mixture of xenophobia and statesmanship, avoided the use of foreign workers in building up its economy, Saudi Arabia is an immigrants' country par excellence. The indigenous population probably numbers no more than 5.0 million as against 1.5 to 2.0 million foreigners. About half of these are Yemenis; the rest are Egyptians, Sudanese, Palestinians, Syrians, Lebanese, and other nationalities. Yemenis do most of the heavy unskilled labor; Egyptians, Syrians, Pakistanis, and others perform the skilled, supervisory, and medium-level technical jobs; Americans and Europeans fill the top-level managerial and technical positions;

Saudi Arabians hold the leading posts in defense, the administration, public management, and other government bureaus.

In terms of brick, mortar, and cement, the Saudi Arabian achievement has been impressive. Construction teams have built postal facilities, factories, and airfields; the face of Saudi Arabia has been profoundly changed. Nevertheless, a large portion of Saudi Arabia's national wealth has gone to arms and prestige projects. The National Development Plan, designed to diversify the country's economy, has had to be modified. Plans to create a heavy industry have been discarded, partly because of marketing problems, partly because heat, dust, and saline water supplies shorten the life of industrial plants and equipment. Saudi Arabia has to battle against serious inflation and against the ills that go with a swollen premodern bureaucracy.

The Palestinian issue   Like prerevolutionary Iran, Saudi Arabia has also to contend with a rapid rate of urbanization and with serious discontent in its labor force. Thousands of students have gone abroad to study, but upon their return they share in running the country. The Palestinians—over a hundred thousand of them in Saudi Arabia—are likewise discontented; the PLO has many adherents within the Palestinian community. Some 60 to 65 percent of Aramco's workers are Palestinians. These have recently been excluded from key positions but, properly organized, they could play a major part in sabotaging the oil fields. The Saudis have therefore been drawn into the Palestinian struggle, even against their will, and they fear another Arab-Israeli war in which the United States will side with the Israelis while the PLO and its allies will press Saudi Arabia to align itself with the Arabs. By spring 1980, the Palestinian issue had even split the Saudi establishment. The pro-American group was led by the powerful Sudairy family; the Arab nationalist or "pro-Arab" faction looked to the Shomar family. Both sides saw the United States as the key to the future of the Middle East because of its increasing dependence on oil and its special links to Israel. The pro-Americans wished to continue cultivating the United States and to provide oil. The pro-Arab group favored lower production of oil and rapprochement with Iraq and other Arab states. In addition, a substantial number of Saudi dignitaries, including King Khalid himself, look to Western Europe as a balancing factor. But if there is not enough progress in the West Bank and Gaza Strip negotiations, the pro-Arabs might well take over.

The defense dilemma   The Saudi Arabian government, like the old Austro-Hungarian monarchy, might be described as despotism softened by incompetence. There is no parliament and no formal constitution. The king serves both as chief of state and head of government; he is his own prime minister and minister for foreign affairs. There are over four thousand Saudi princes who derive their income from the civil list; they are among the truest supporters of monarchy, as are the great families—the Sudairis and the as-Sheikhs—who helped the Saudis overrun most of the Arabian Peninsula in the 1920s. The bedouin population, traditional supporters of the monarchy, is declining numerically and cannot serve as the permanent basis of the state.

Saudi Arabia, like most of the other Arab nations, for the moment has no scientific and technological infrastructure. Most Saudis lack a proper understanding of science and technology; they will not find it easy to make intelligent choices regarding what technology to import and how it should best be adapted to local conditions and needs. The Saudis will continue to depend on foreign experts in most fields for several decades. There is the danger that such developments as do occur—for instance, in the oil industry and associated enterprises—will not lead to wider structural change. The Saudi rulers are in a cleft stick. Unless they take active steps to institutionalize science and technology and allow for structural change in their society, the oil money will have been wasted—just as the Iberian monarchies wasted the gold from the New World.[4] But if they proceed too fast, Saudi society will not be able to take the strain and the monarchy will surely collapse.

Saudi Arabia also feels threatened by the advance of Marxism in countries as diverse as Ethiopia, Afghanistan, and South Yemen. At the same time, the Saudis are menaced by internal unrest. Since the collapse of the Iranian monarchy, they have launched an extensive military program. King Khalid City is being developed as a great military base in the middle of the desert, designed to accommodate sixty thousand troops, seventy thousand support personnel, and units of combat aircraft. Four more bases like it will be spread throughout the Arabian Peninsula to enable the Saudi army to move swiftly from one part of the country to the other. The regular army, including many officers trained in the United States, will increase from sixty-one thousand to a hundred thousand. The National Guard, organized for protecting the regime and guarding the oil fields, will grow from forty thousand to seventy-five thousand men. The French have agreed to equip three armored brigades with modern tanks; they will also install a new air-defense system. The United States has agreed to sell vast supplies of military equipment to the Saudi army, as well as F-15s to the Saudi air force. Pakistani troops have been stationed in the country.

The Saudi army nevertheless faces difficult problems. These range from preparing for possible regular military operations against Soviet proxy troops to combating sabotage in the oil fields; from coping with Palestinian operations designed to endanger navigation of the Strait of Hormuz to engaging in counterinsurgency actions against the Popular Front for the Liberation of Oman, based in South Yemen. The rapid military buildup may well create social and economic difficulties, as it did in Iran. The regular forces, recruited mainly in the cities, cannot be isolated from the effects of general urban discontent. The National Guard, who are mostly tribesmen, shares the grievances of the tribesmen now being drawn into the cities. Saudi Arabia is deficient in the technological skills needed to operate modern weapons systems and suffers from a general manpower shortage. Its indigenous population is small. The Saudis have therefore decided to introduce conscription.

A Prerevolutionary Situation?

Can Saudi Arabia avoid a revolution like the one in Iran? The country has serious weaknesses. Members of the Saudi upper class, with great financial stakes as far afield as Texas and California, widely lack a sense of commitment to their country. The nation has to contend with discontent among immigrants, especially Palestinians, with urban unrest, and with dissension among the bedouins being drawn into the cities. On the other hand, Saudi Arabia's population is much smaller than Iran's; hence a larger share of the oil wealth trickles down to the people. Saudi Arabia's Sunni tradition lacks the potentially revolutionary appeal of the Shi'ite creed in Iran; despite Shi'ite unrest, Saudi Arabia is unlikely to experience a revolution in which the clergy are prominent. The Saudi monarchy eschews secularism but wisely rules through Islam in a manner that commands wide popular support. Saudi Arabia's ethnic problems are nothing like as serious as Iran's. Nevertheless, the Saudis will require statesmanship on the highest level to steer their ship of state through the present storm.

In dealing with Saudi Arabia, the United States has made many mistakes similar to those committed in its contacts with Iran. There is the danger that Saudi Arabia may be armed beyond its capacity. Americans must recognize that the ancien régime in Saudi Arabia is likely to be unstable. But we do have a vital interest in its reformation, and we must be willing to help the Saudis to modernize sensibly. At the same time, we need to aid them in defending both their security and their oil production, elements essential to the well-being of the West. We cannot tolerate either an attack on Saudi Arabia through Soviet proxies or a prolonged shutdown of the Saudi oil industry. We should attempt to work out a concerted strategy with Japan and the Western European countries; these nations are even more vulnerable to the disruption of the Middle Eastern oil supplies than we are. Such a policy will require an informed and determined public opinion as well as military forces adequate to the task. We should be wary of a Maginot Line strategy that concentrates solely on a frontal defense of Western Europe while ignoring the possibility of a flank attack on its oil supplies.

We should share our military responsibilities among our allies. For example, let the British be responsible for defense of the Persian Gulf and the French care for the Horn of Africa and the Indian Ocean. We do not want to Americanize the protection of the Gulf and the Arabian Peninsula; rather, let us share responsibility for protecting this vital area.

TURKEY

Turkey, once the core of a great monarchy dominating southeastern Europe and most of the Mediterranean Sea, lost its empire in 1919. Yet it remains a powerful state, the most important military power in the Near East. Turkey's area is large, some three hundred thousand square miles; its population exceeds forty million. Ethnically, Turkey used to be a most heterogeneous country. But its Armenian community was largely destroyed during World War I, in a brutal holocaust that antedated the persecution of the Jews in Europe, and its once-influential Greek minority was expelled after the desperate war of 1921–22 against Greece. Today the majority of the population speaks Turkish as its mother tongue.

The largest minority is made up of Kurds—officially known as "Mountain Turks"—who may number as many as nine million. The Kurds have four million kinsmen across the border in Iran and another three million in Iraq. The Kurdish question is a longstanding one. The Treaty of Sèvres (1920) imposed on Turkey by the victorious Allies after World War I actually provided for the creation of a Kurdish state; this requirement was omitted from the Treaty of Lausanne (1923), which took the place of the former agreement. The Kurds are predominantly a rural people; many of them remain backward, but national sentiment continues to grow as education advances in the villages. Iraq and Iran have both had to cope with armed resistance from the Kurds, and the

FIGURE 4.3 TURKEY

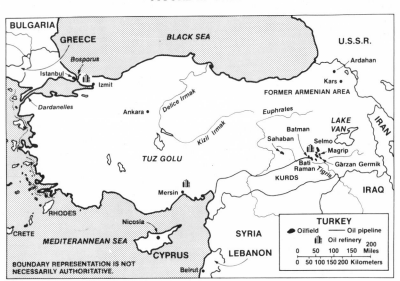

1980s will surely see an intensification of the Kurdish question. Turkey, Iraq, and Iran have a common interest in preventing the emergence of an independent Kurdish state, but all will have to cope with a continued Kurdish problem within their borders.

From the economic standpoint, Turkey has many assets. The country is rich in minerals and has a potentially large supply of hydroelectric power, but these resources remain to be developed. Westernization has swiftly accelerated since Kemal Atatürk's harsh but competent rule as president from 1923 to 1938, and in economic terms the Turkish achievement has been impressive. The Turkish road and rail network is the best in the Middle East. Turkish agricultural production, dependent almost entirely on peasant enterprise and not on great landowners, has considerably increased over the last twenty years. Since the 1950s Turkey has gone through an industrial revolution and the growth of its GNP has been striking. The nation today has important textile industries. Petrochemical engineering, motor vehicle production (assembly and parts manufacturing), rubber, plastics, iron and steel, food processing, cement, building materials, etc., account for a large part of the national wealth, and Turkish industries will continue to expand their production.

Many economic problems remain. Agriculture, accounting for nearly 70 percent of the country's employed population but less than 30 percent of its national income, is still backward and undercapitalized, the stepchild of official planning. Turkey has to contend with a huge bureaucracy and a widely inefficient system of state intervention in economic affairs. The State Planning Organization, set up in 1960, controls all major Turkish private and state investments and wields far-reaching powers regarding foreign investments; the state provides a large share of all fixed capital investments—more than 50 percent in 1970. Turkey never quite recovered from the sudden rise in world oil prices in 1973/74. This intensified existing economic problems, and the nation has teetered on the brink of bankruptcy ever since. As prices of imported raw materials have gone up, the new Turkish industries have found themselves at an increasing disadvantage. The rate of inflation in 1978 has been estimated at 40 percent per annum. There have been recurrent deficits in the balance of payments; since 1970 the foreign debt has tripled, reaching $12 billion early in 1979. At that time nearly half the country's plant capacity lay unused; there were shortages of everything from light bulbs to traditional Turkish coffee; electrical stoppages were common, and industrial unrest was widespread. These ills were made worse by the bureaucratic shortcomings described above.

Turkey has one of the highest birth rates in the world; nearly two-thirds of the population are under thirty years of age. Like Iran, the country must find jobs for an ever-growing number of young people. Migrants from the villages crowd into the cities or try to find work in Western Europe, especially in West

Germany and Switzerland. There is a high rate of urbanization with all its attendant ills, and there are striking contrasts between city and countryside. Unemployment in 1978 supposedly struck 20 percent of the labor force. Merchants, professional men, and technicians, like unskilled workers, have begun to leave Turkey's shores. By 1979 Turkey was divided by bitter violence. Rival gangs of youthful militants, right and left, were conducting running feuds; political terrorism was widespread. There were clashes between Sunni Muslims—the majority, who tend to be right-wing in their political orientation—and the Shi'ite minority, who are inclined to sympathize with left-wingers. In 1978 and 1979 rioting led to the imposition of martial law in most of the country's sixty-seven provinces—a serious blow to a once-peaceful country.

The riots were suppressed, but Turkey remains unstable. Civil strife will continue to threaten it until political stability returns and the country can solve its economic problems—inflation, unemployment, trade deficits, foreign debts. By 1978 Prime Minister Bülent Ecevit's coalition government was under heavy pressure from critics within parliament and from the extraparliamentary opposition, an opposition that included militant strikers and was drawn from both the extreme left and the extreme right ranks of the intelligentsia. In November 1979 Süleyman Demirel's Justice Party formed a minority government that continued to be troubled by the activities of leftist, Kurdish, and Armenian dissidents, as well as by parliamentary fractionalism. As a result, Turkey drifted into a lengthy period of indecision, and the military intervened in September 1980. An uneasy order was imposed.

Turkey's domestic problems are paralleled by difficulties in its foreign policy. Its neighbor the Soviet Union has traditionally laid claim to control of the Turkish Straits (Dardanelles) and in 1945 laid claim to Turkish territory in the Caucasus and along the Black Sea. But Turkey's most immediate problems relate to Greece and Cyprus. Both are troublesome issues that, willy-nilly, have involved the United States in quarrels not of its making. The major disagreement concerns control over the continental shelf in the Aegean Sea. This quarrel began in 1974, when oil was discovered at the island of Thasos (which lies off the coast of Macedonia and does not form part of the continental shelf). Turkey then laid claim to large portions of the continental shelf. The quarrel between the two nations was envenomed by the Arab oil boycott of 1973, which increased pressure both on Turkey and Greece to find alternative sources of energy. Greece demanded that the issue should be referred to the International Court of Justice at the Hague. Turkey insisted that it would not be bound by any international court ruling as it had not signed the Geneva Convention of 1958 concerning mineral exploration on each nation's continental shelf. Greece considered the Turkish division of the Aegean to be arbitrary; Greeks were profoundly disturbed—and rightly so—when Turkish statesmen challenged Greek rights to the Dodecanese and other islands. The Turks created an Aegean Army to back their claims. There were bitter disputes concerning the NATO command in the Aegean, air traffic control in the Aegean, and other matters of major concern to NATO. Turkey for a time opposed the reintegration of Greece into NATO, which was accomplished only in 1980.

The Cyprus Issue and US Policy

The most serious Turko-Greek dispute, however, concerns the island of Cyprus. Both sides can make a good claim. The great majority of the Cypriot population speak Greek; many Cypriots would welcome *enosis* (union) with Greece. Cyprus, though never a part of the modern Kingdom of Greece, has formed part of the Hellenic world since antiquity. In the Turkish view, however, *enosis* would be a gross violation of Turkish minority rights. After being an Ottoman possession for three centuries, Cyprus came under British administration in 1878, a domination challenged by Greek partisans in the 1950s. After lengthy negotiations between Turkey, Greece, Great Britain, and the newly formed Republic of Cyprus, the Treaty of London was concluded in 1960 to give special protection to the island's Turkish minority, about one-quarter of the population. The signatories guaranteed the Cyprus constitution, and each of the three guaranteeing powers—Turkey, Greece, and Great Britain—reserved "the right to take action" if the treaty were broken.

The Turkish minority was exposed to constant harassment during the 1960s and early 1970s. There was bitter intercommunal strife in which the Americans essentially sided with the Greeks. Greek Cypriots unilaterally changed the Cyprus constitution in 1963. Greece infiltrated military personnel onto the island, and made life miserable for the Turks so as to speed their departure. In 1974 the Cypriot National Guard, a Greek body, overthrew the government of Archbishop Makarios, and Nikos Sampson, a former guerrilla leader who had previously been condemned to death by the British for his activities, assumed the presidency. Stung to the quick, the Turks invaded the island and established Turkish authority over something like 40 percent of Cyprus. The Greeks in this region, after much suffering, sought refuge in the Greek zone.

The Turks then consolidated their authority by sending more Turkish settlers to the disputed territory. They later set up a Turkish Federated State of Cyprus, thereby giving the Turkish community and its leaders an institutional stake in the status quo, which included a continuing Turkish military presence. The Greeks performed a minor economic miracle in their part of the island; most refugees were resettled and found work. But the Greeks insisted that partition was no answer, that the island's economy could not recover if Cyprus were to be divided by an iron curtain, and that the two communities should be united within a federal government. In 1977 Makarios and the Turkish Cypriot leader Rauf Dentash agreed to a compromise solution, but the agreement broke down in practice, each side blaming the United States as well as each other.

In retaliation for the Turks' action in Cyprus the Greek-American lobby, intelligent and well-organized but misguided, induced Congress to impose an arms embargo against Turkey in 1975. The embargo was later partially rescinded and was lifted altogether in 1978. But its consequences in Turko-American relations were disastrous. American military men were evicted from five important intelligence-gathering bases; the Turkish armed forces, denied additional equipment, suffered in their military preparedness, thus weakening their position in NATO. In 1977 the Turks began to improve their relations with the Soviet Union, soon to become Turkey's principal source of investment capital. In order to balance existing commitments to the United States and the European Economic Community, the Turks formed closer ties with Eastern Europe and with the Islamic countries of the Middle East.

From the US standpoint the embargo was a serious error. Turkey, for all its numerous troubles, was not likely to become another Iran. Turkey was not subject to an absolute monarchy as was prerevolutionary Iran. The Turks had an elected parliament and a relatively free press. In constitutional liberties, only Iran could compare with Turkey. There was no mass movement seeking to overthrow the Turkish political system as there was in Iran. Muslim fundamentalism was much less powerful than it was in Iran, as was the influence of conservative Muslim divines. Turkish society was much more secular in character than that of Iran; the dominant Sunni did not on the whole incline toward radicalism; Turkey's economy was relatively advanced; Turkey's middle class was much more substantial than Iran's and modernization had gone a great deal further. In many ways Turkey resembled an Eastern European state more than a Middle Eastern state.

The Turkish parliamentary regime unfortunately was unable to solve the country's political and social problems. At the end of 1979 the conservative Justice Party, headed by Süleyman Demirel, took over from Ecevit's Republican People's Party which had ruled the country since 1978. Demirel, however, could not cope with the rising tide of political violence between members of extreme right-wing and extreme left-wing terrorists. Between 1975 and 1980, more than 4,000 persons had lost their lives in frays and assassinations. The economy, while slowly recovering, remained the weakest in the Western alliance. Demirel's government found itself virtually paralyzed owing to its dependence on its coalition partner in parliament, a militant Muslim party, which advocated support for revolutionary Iran, breaking ties with Israel, and a policy of aloofness toward the EEC.

In September 1980 the army reluctantly seized power. Many political leaders, including Ecevit and Demirel, were arrested; martial law was extended throughout the country; parliament, all political parties, and all political associations were dissolved. The army faced an extremely difficult task. The repression of terrorist activity is a police, not a military, problem. Although the army has proved more effective than the civilian authorities in dealing with assassins, the army is ill-fitted to run the government or the economy; sooner or later, the generals will have to draw on civilian skills. Nevertheless, the United States should support Turkey, on the grounds that a military regime is a lesser evil than civil war or breakdown of government.

In its international relations, the United States must balance its interests in Greece and Turkey. Greco-American ties are rightly valued by Washington. But however important, they must not predominate over Turko-American relations in the wider calculation of US interests and Western interests as a whole. The Greco-Turkish quarrel presents the United States with an almost insoluble dilemma, for there is much to be said on either side. Greece and Turkey, moreover, are strategically interdependent; NATO cannot risk losing either one of its two hostile allies. If the United States sides in too open a fashion with Turkey, Greece might be forced into a neutralist position. The strategic effects for Turkey would be disastrous, for an isolated Turkey—unable to rely on assistance from Greek naval and air bases—would be almost indefensible. The defection of Greece from the NATO alliance would also endanger Italy's strategic position in the Mediterranean. In terms of numbers, the Greek armed forces are much inferior to Turkey's (190,000 as against 485,000 men, in 1978/79). But Greek military expenditure is not much inferior to Turkey's ($1.25 billion as against $1.7 billion in 1978), and what the Greeks lack in numbers they make up for in technical efficiency. The Greek and Turkish forces have complementary roles; unfortunately, both alliance partners are now more apt to glower at each other than to look over their shoulders at the more distant Soviet threat.

The United States, in its own interest, must take as much account of Turkey as of Greece. Turkey's strategic position is as important to this country as is Turkish power. Turkey controls the exit from the Black Sea to the Bosporus as well as entry to the Aegean Sea through the Dardanelles. The country plays an essential part in NATO by providing a large number of strategic bases for combat, navigation, communications, and intelligence operations. The Turkish armed forces, which proved their combat efficacy in the Korean War, total nearly half a million men—far more than the Greek forces. Their cooperation is essential to the defense of the eastern Mediterranean against the Soviet Union and to NATO's defense of its southern flank. Turkish friendship is also essential to the defense of the Persian Gulf. Provided the Soviets can be permitted to overfly Turkish airspace at will, they can cut in half the time they need to deploy forces by air in the Persian Gulf, Syria, or Lebanon. In the event of a crisis, Soviet airborne forces could reach these threatened areas well before US forces of equivalent size.

From the Greek standpoint, close US-Turkish relations are also essential. Turkey's participation in NATO greatly increases the Greek homeland's security. Turkish control of the Dardanelles blocks the Soviet sealanes, making the Soviet Mediterranean fleet more vulnerable to NATO air forces and hampering any efforts by the Soviet navy to support land forces engaged in an attack on Greece. If the Turkish armed forces were neutralized, the Soviets would be able to increase the number of troops stationed on the central front and would make NATO's position in Central Europe even more difficult than it is at the moment.

Given these elementary military facts, US policy toward Turkey has been offensively moralistic in form, fumbling and inept in content. The United States is no longer trusted by the Turks as a steadfast ally. In 1979, while remaining a member of NATO, Turkey made moves toward the radical Arab camp. Ecevit withdrew from the Central Treaty Organization and asked for its formal dissolution, Iran and Pakistan having already abrogated their membership.

Turkey's motives were not hard to fathom: it did not wish to be regarded by the Arab powers as the sole Western outpost in the region; it also looked to the Arab countries for economic benefits. Iraq and Libya supply most of Turkey's oil and have now agreed to extend credits and to buy more Turkish goods. Having experienced diplomatic slights and difficulties in obtaining loans from the West, Turkey has turned to the radical Arab states and can be counted on to pursue an anti-Israeli and pro-Palestinian policy. The first task of the United States in the Middle East must then be to restore the Turkish alliance, which should form the keystone of US policy in the eastern Mediterranean. A Turko-American rapprochement will test the diplomats' skill. There is no Turkish lobby to counter the Greek lobby in the United States, yet Turko-American understanding is essential to the future of Greece as well as of Turkey.

Turkey, unfortunately, faces very serious problems. As a result of our ill-considered embargo, the Turkish armed forces—trained according to American specifications—are now dependent on obsolescent equipment. For strategic and ethnic reasons alike, eastern Turkey is almost indefensible. The Turkish armed forces, moreover, face serious social problems, some of which have been aggravated by the nature of US military advice. Few sergeants are advanced into the officer corps; hence relations between commissioned and noncommissioned officers leave much to be desired. In accordance with American counsel, the Turks abolished the old-fashioned military schools that had enabled sons of peasants and shopkeepers to rise into the commissioned ranks and make a name for themselves. The college graduates now serving in the ranks enjoy a special status. They supply the bulk of the officers; most of them are of middle-class origin, remote in life style and outlook from the ordinary recruits drawn from among the workers and the peasantry. Even in the civilian

sphere, American help has had unintended strategic consequences of an undesirable kind. For instance, US aid has contributed to the construction of an
excellent highway system. Unfortunately, the Turks have therefore neglected
their railway system and turned to using more cars and trucks, thereby increasing their dependence on imported oil at a time of rising scarcity.

Turkey remains a strongly nationalistic and sometimes even a xenophobic
country. The secular revolution is not likely to be undone. The army has no
avowed political ambitions. But suspicion of foreigners militates against foreign investment. America's reputation, especially, has sunk to a low ebb, partly
because of the wavering, inconsistent, and often even incomprehensible nature
of our foreign policy, partly also because the Turks initially had unrealistic
expectations of the benefits to be derived from the American alliance. Neu-
tralism makes sense, not only to those Turks who sympathize with the Soviet
Union, but also to many of the younger Turkish reserve officers who regard
their country as indefensible in conventional military terms, and who would
prefer to resist a possible Russian attack by preplanned guerrilla warfare.
They have a point. What is the object of relying on an American alliance that
invites Soviet hostility, and that seems to bend at every turn to equally hostile
ethnic lobbies in Washington?

There are also the country's economic problems, which cannot wait. The
1980s will determine whether or not Turkey can solve these problems under a
democratic government or whether it will stay with an inefficient form of military rule. The rulers of Turkey face a difficult task: they have to stop internecine violence, improve the economy, limit wasteful and inefficient public
enterprise, stimulate exports, encourage tourism, and develop mineral resources—all this while limiting the country's present high rate of population
growth.

Even if Turkey does not succeed in all these difficult tasks, however, the
United States, in its own interests, should support this valuable ally by all
possible means. Turkey is too important to NATO to be allowed to founder or
to drift into revolution. We should therefore assist Turkey with grants and
other forms of aid. We should encourage the West German government to
continue and enlarge the financial assistance it has so wisely given to Turkey.
We must also be careful not to kill the patient by insisting on unsuitable cures.
The West should help the Turkish government put an end to internal violence
and surmount its economic problems. However unpopular foreign aid has become in Turkey, even $1 billion a year may be a small price to pay to keep it
within the orbit of the West. The United States, at the same time, should
encourage Greeks and Turks alike to arrive at a peaceful solution of their disputes. Greece and Turkey are both convinced, unfortunately, that he who pays
the piper calls the tune; neither side appreciates that American leverage ex-
erted through foreign aid is limited, or that the piper—once paid—prefers to

play his own melody. Washington can, however, point out to both sides that all NATO members are faced by a growing Soviet threat, and that mutual accommodation will serve the self-interest of Greece and Turkey alike. Instead of inviting dislike through public adjuration and ill-preached sermons, we in the United States should act through quiet and tactful diplomacy; we should express our preferences in terms of realpolitik and our own national interests, instead of offending both sides through an unwarranted assumption of moral superiority.

5

US Special Interests

Oil is the lifeblood of the modern world; it fuels petro-chemical industries, heats houses, activates factories, ships, cars, and planes. Oil is a major implement of war as well as of peace. Only a generation ago the United States accounted for nearly three-quarters of the world's oil output. In 1977 the US share had fallen to less than one-seventh, even though the nation remained one of the world's largest individual producers (see table 5.1). By the 1970s the United States, the world's largest oil consumer, had also turned into the world's largest oil importer. For the next two decades, the primary growth market for Middle Eastern oil will be the American one.[1] The importance of oil from the Middle East will be all the greater because America's major allies—the industrialized countries of Western Europe as well as Japan—are even more dependent on uninterrupted supplies from that area than is America itself.

THE PROBLEM OF OIL

According to the optimists, found especially among the advocates of free enterprise, the so-called energy problem in the United States is not a problem at all. The world's resources have always been scarce. Only utopians and fools, the optimists say, could possibly believe that mankind has ever lived in a state of poverty amidst plenty. Insofar as there is an energy shortage, they continue, it has been artificially manufactured by government intervention. They also blame the environmental opponents of nuclear power, whose indignation, they allege, is aimed selectively at nuclear power installations in the Western world but rarely at those located on the other side of the Iron Curtain.

The optimists claim that the energy problems of the future are not too hard to solve. If the US government were to do away with its unnecessary control of the oil industry, its equally unnecessary environmental controls, and its minimum price laws for natural gas and other energy sources, the price mechanisms of the free market would soon induce energy producers to produce more. The present crisis is no crisis at all, to the optimists. The world's potential oil resources are vast. As oil prices rise, new oil wells in the North Sea, in Mexico, the coastal waters of the United States, of China, and elsewhere, would soon make up any shortfalls.

Rising oil prices, the optimists continue, may be a blessing rather than a curse. As prices rise, we shall reduce excessive oil consumption by making more effective use of electric motors, by driving less, by restricting oil use to its essential functions, by ceasing to overlight and to overheat our rooms, and by other such conservation measures. The United States has vast supplies of domestic coal. There is no reason why we should not, like South Africa, meet a

TABLE 5.1
WORLD CRUDE OIL PRODUCTION, JULY 1979
(preliminary figures)

Region	Production (thousand barrels per day)
Free world	48,930
Western hemisphere	15,305
United States	8,625
Canada	1,525
Mexico	1,415
Venezuela	2,330
Argentina	470
Western Europe	2,370
Middle East (excl. N. Africa)	21,985
Bahrein	50
Iraq	3,050
Kuwait	40
Neutral Zone	2,275
Oman	295
Qatar	520
Saudi Arabia	9,500
United Arab Emirates	1,835
Iran	3,750
Africa	6,365
Algeria	900
Libya	2,080
Nigeria	2,380
Angola	900
Asia-Pacific	2,905
Communist countries	14,160
USSR	11,400
China	2,280
Romania	300
WORLD	**63,090**

SOURCE: *International Energy Statistical Review*, 31 Oct. 1979, p. 1.

large portion of our domestic needs by turning coal into oil. Sooner or later engineers will work out blueprints for new forms of energy derived from oil shale and nuclear, solar, or tidal power. New ways will also be found to economize on existing forms of fuel. Hydrogen, methanol, and other substitutes could help to remedy the shortage of fossil fuels provided that research and manufacturing receive adequate support. By the end of the 1980s, therefore, planners may well have to deal with problems occasioned by an oil glut rather than with a global oil shortage.

Unjustified fear for the future, the optimists claim, has created a number of myths about the present. We have, for instance, outrageous misconceptions concerning the supposed unfairness of Arab oil producers. The price rise of the 1970s was not a piece of blackmail on their part; rather, it merely made up for the present inflation of the dollar and for the unreasonably low prices charged during the 1960s, when oil consumers got accustomed to paying little more than the production costs in return for crude oil. Oil sheikhs as portrayed in the American press often serve as convenient scapegoats for the deficiencies of our own policy makers. Contrary to a widespread misapprehension, the international oil producers, for instance, are not responsible for worldwide inflation.

Inflation, the argument continues, had been well underway in the West before the oil price hike of the 1970s. Inflation was brought about by factors quite unrelated to OPEC policies—the expense of the Vietnam war, American unwillingness to pay for the cost of that war by higher taxation, the growing level of public expenditure for peaceful purposes in the West, and the excessive expansion of the money supply in the United States and abroad. Contrary to many predictions, the international monetary system did not collapse because of rising oil prices. The industrially advanced economies were not taken over by a financial conspiracy of rich oil sheikhs. Oil prices did not rise unduly when compared to the rise in costs of manufactured materials. Compared with the GNPs of the world's major industrialized countries, the GNPs of the oil-producing countries remained puny.

The pessimists look upon the future in a very different fashion. They view with apprehension the unprecedented power that has suddenly accrued to weak and backward states like Saudi Arabia, Kuwait, and Libya. Between them, the OPEC powers now control a major share of a vital resource without which, the pessimists feel, the Western economies would collapse. According to some of the pessimists, the sudden oil embargo engineered by the Arabs during the Arab-Israeli war of 1973, with the subsequent price increases, has caused financial strains so severe as to plunge the world into inflation and recession. The pessimists claim that OPEC plays a nefarious role in the world economy. By 1977 the OPEC countries had accumulated at least $150 billion in financial reserves and liquid assets, giving them an enormous degree of financial power. The Western position will deteriorate even further if these vast resources are permitted to come under Soviet influence, by indirect or direct means. In the event of such a catastrophe the Soviet Union would exercise a stranglehold over both Western Europe and Japan and would be able to control the greatest industrial aggregations in the world outside the United States.

In terms of dependency, the pessimists paint an even gloomier picture for the West. By 1975 the major consuming countries had come to rely heavily on Arab oil (see table 5.2). The Arab states, collectively at least, had become a world power. The Western countries' changing attitudes towards Israel were linked to their reliance on oil.

Protecting US Interests

Over the long run we side with the optimists in this argument. We see no reason why Arab oil producers should not charge for their product what the market will bear, as do the producers of any other merchandise for sale. Many Westerners have expressed their fear—bordering at times on panic—concerning the enormous reserve of petrodollars accumulated by Arab oil producers. If not "recycled" into the world monetary system, these reserves supposedly could undermine the world economy. These fears have proved unfounded in practice. By 1978 even Saudi Arabia, which had accumulated foreign reserves worth about $60 billion, was beginning to experience a liquidity crisis and was drawing on her reserves to meet short-term financial obligations.[2]

US energy problems of the future will be much influenced by what Ameri-

TABLE 5.2

SELECTED CONSUMING COUNTRIES' DEPENDENCE ON IMPORTED OIL, 1975

(in percent of imports)

Country	Arab Oil (percent)	Non-Arab Oil (percent)
United States	29.9	70.6
Japan	50.7	49.3
Canada	33.7	66.3
Western Europe (total)	62.3	37.7
Great Britain	54.1	45.9
West Germany	59.4	40.6
Italy	71.1	28.6
France	70.8	29.2
Netherlands	48.3	51.7
Belgium-Luxemburg	50.8	49.2
Spain	70.77	29.3

SOURCE: "The Middle East: US Policy," *Congressional Quarterly* (Washington DC, 1977), p. 126.

cans do in their own country to solve problems that have little to do with the Middle East. Among the issues that Washington will have to decide are federal pollution standards, price controls, and regulations of the oil, transportation, and related industries. The future will also be shaped by the ability of Western inventors and entrepreneurs to develop new forms of power. There is a great deal, moreover, that the United States can do now with its existing resources; for instance, it can learn to use energy in a more efficient and less wasteful manner, it can scale down inflation, and it can reduce bureaucratic interference with the working of the economy, especially in the production of domestic oil.

Over the short run, however, we are pessimists. The availability of new energy supplies during the 1980s will be greatly influenced by the amount of time needed to develop alternatives. By 1976 the lead time needed to produce oil from proven but as yet inoperative fields was estimated at two years for the Middle East and three to seven years for the United States. In the United States as elsewhere, oil from new fields in frontier areas without proven productive capacities takes five to seven years from discovery of the field to production. The lead time for nuclear power plants is reckoned at between seven and nine years. Gasification of coal, used at present on a large scale only in South Africa, requires ten to fifteen years.

For the immediate future the Western world also faces other snags. Production from the North Sea, in which British and Norwegian policy makers place such hopes, will actually be limited to an estimated four million barrels per day by the 1980s. Expansion of nuclear energy in general has been slowed significantly, especially in the United States, because of rising costs and increasing public concern about safety standards. Expanded coal production also faces problems, even though the price of coal as fuel has risen considerably since the late 1960s. The use of coal as fuel for electric power poses environmental problems because much of the coal mined in the eastern United States has a high sulfur content. The best low-sulfur coal comes from the western part of the country and is expensive to transport eastwards. Coal liquefaction and gasification processes are expensive and so—for the moment—are synthetic fuels derived from coal.

During the 1980s, then, the Western nations cannot do without large supplies of Middle Eastern oil. If the West is to survive economically and politically, Middle Eastern oil wells, especially those around the Persian Gulf and in Saudi Arabia, cannot be permitted to pass under communist control. The United States should attempt in its own self-interest to maintain the Middle East as a Western zone and to protect its oil supplies. This would best be achieved by skillful diplomacy, by strengthening local military forces, and by stabilizing local governments while helping them to modernize cautiously. In an extreme emergency the United States and its Western allies may have to intervene to help Saudi Arabia and the Persian Gulf states. Should the Soviet Union attempt to interfere, either directly or through Cuban and East German proxies, we and the NATO powers should respond by armed force. Our determination to intervene in the event of such extreme emergencies must be stated clearly and unambiguously by the president. We must develop an equally stern resolve to disregard the strictures of pacifists and fellow travelers, no matter whether they come from Congress, colleges, lecture rooms, or churches.

NATO intervention should take place, if possible, in concert with such friendly Arab powers as Egypt or Saudi Arabia. It will require an expansion of NATO's airlift capacity and the availability of highly trained mobile divisions. Military power should also be used in the event of attempted internal subversion in the gulf states or Saudi Arabia or of an oil boycott instituted for political purposes. Such policies will commend themselves neither to the morally righteous nor to radicals, but they are essential to the West's survival. We must show the will and acquire the means for such interventions in order to blunt radical takeovers or Soviet expansionism.[3]

For this purpose the United States should develop adequate strategy and contingency plans to move an effective fighting force into the area. In spring 1980 the United States had four units of the army's strategic reserve available for use in the Middle East. (These comprised, according to the *New York Times*, the 82nd Airborne and the 101st Air Assault Division at Fort Bragg, North Carolina; the First Cavalry Division, an armored unit, at Fort Hood, Texas; the Ninth Infantry Division at Fort Lewis, Washington; and the Second Marine Division and its supporting air wing stationed at Camp Lejeune, North Carolina.) Given the limited strength of these forces, as well as the logistic difficulties of deploying them, they would have a hard time resisting a major Soviet assault supported by massive airpower and armor. The Soviet Union was far ahead in this respect, with extensive stockpiles of weapons (both light and heavy), ammunition, spare parts, and other material distributed as far afield as Libya, Syria, Iraq, Ethiopia, and South Yemen. In order to intervene successfully our forces require more air transport, a network of prepositioned bases, fuel and ammunition dumps, spare parts, repair facilities, airstrips, and accommodations for troops—all available for use at short notice. These facilities would best be located in the Sinai or in Saudi Arabia, in addition to the ones already planned for Oman, Somalia, and Kenya.

American and NATO diplomats have the difficult task of persuading Saudi Arabia that a US or NATO promise of support can be relied upon, and that Saudi Arabia must further collaborate with the West in case the Soviets gain a military advantage that cannot be undone. The Saudis must be convinced that we intend to stop the Soviet advance and that we will stand by our friends.

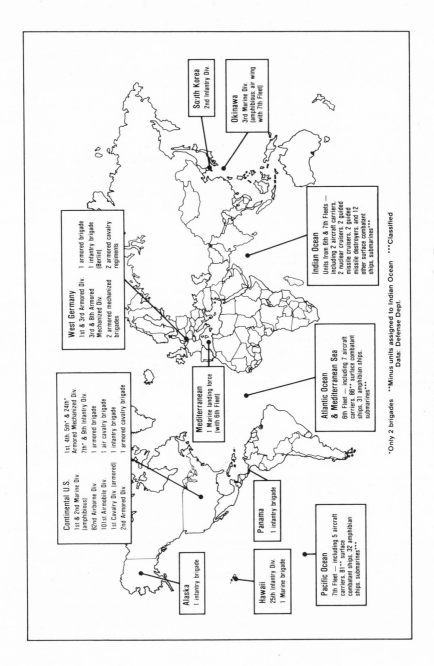

South Korea
2nd Infantry Div.

Okinawa
3rd Marine Div.
(amphibious; air wing
with 7th Fleet)

West Germany
1st & 3rd Armored Div.   1 armored brigade
7th* & 9th Infantry Div.   1 infantry brigade
3rd & 8th Armored   (Berlin)
Mechanized Div.   2 armored cavalry
2 armored mechanized   regiments
brigades

Indian Ocean
Units from 6th & 7th Fleets —
including 2 aircraft carriers,
2 nuclear cruisers, 2 guided
missile cruisers, 2 guided
missile destroyers, and 12
other surface combatant
ships, submarines***

Continental U.S.
1st, 4th, 5th* & 24th*
Armored Mechanized Div.
82nd Airborne Div.   1 armored brigade
101st Airmobile Div.   1 air cavalry brigade
1st Cavalry Div. (armored)   1 infantry brigade
2nd Armored Div.   1 armored cavalry brigade

Mediterranean
1 Marine landing force
(with 6th Fleet)

**Atlantic Ocean
& Mediterranean Sea**
6th Fleet — including 7 aircraft
carriers, 86** surface combatant
ships, 31 amphibian ships,
submarines***

Alaska
1 infantry brigade

Panama
1 infantry brigade

Hawaii
25th Infantry Div.
1 Marine brigade

Pacific Ocean
7th Fleet — including 5 aircraft
carriers, 81** surface
combatant ships, 32 amphibian
ships, submarines***

*Only 2 brigades   **Minus units assigned to Indian Ocean   ***Classified
Data: Defense Dept.

FIGURE 5.1   MAJOR U.S. LAND AND SEA FORCES

RUSSIA AND THE UNITED STATES
IN THE MIDDLE EAST

Throughout the last two centuries the Middle East has been an arena of strife for the Great Powers. Russia, for example, has traditionally sought to extend its boundaries to the south; the British and French intervened there in the nineteenth and twentieth centuries; and the United States sent marines to Lebanon in 1958.

According to Soviet theoreticians, the Soviet Union represents the interests of the world's working class; while the Western nations stand for the power of the bourgeoisie. Conflict between the Soviets and the West is therefore inevitable. Competition for markets, raw materials, or naval bases; peaceful relations through scholarships, trade, and diplomacy; aggression by proxy through strikes, guerrilla campaigns, and wars of liberation; all must serve as revolutionary tools. Peaceful competition can exist for a time between states built on differing social systems, but there can be no peaceful coexistence between contending classes. Détente, to Soviet theoreticians, is but a means of intensifying the global class struggle and assuring the doom of the bourgeoisie. As the Soviets see it, the international balance of forces has shifted in favor of the socialist camp. The balance must be tilted further, and in this struggle the Middle East, with its vast oil resources and numerous conflict situations, plays an essential part. This proposed strategy is receiving greater emphasis because of the possibility that Soviet domestic oil supplies may be diminishing.

The Soviet Union has used various means to advance its ends. In 1945 Moscow called for Soviet control of the Bosporus; in addition, the Soviet Union claimed Turkish territory in the Caucasus and along an extensive stretch of the Turkish Black Sea coast. The Soviets also set up short-lived puppet governments in Azerbaijan, in northern Iran, while communist insurgents attempted to take over Greece.[4] These territorial claims, however, were subsequently abandoned under pressure from the West. The Soviet Union also works through local communist parties, most of which operate in illegality or semilegality. Their membership remains small; their political power is greatest in a "united front," that is, as long as they manage to act as partners within a broader coalition. The Iraqi Communist Party, the best-organized and most disciplined of such parties in the Arab world, established an alliance with the governing Ba'ath Party in 1973 (this did not protect the Communists, however, from subsequent severe persecution). Finally, the Soviet Union seeks advantages of a conventional kind by collaborating with incumbent governments, to which it offers arms and technicians. Through this strategy the Soviets have gained many temporary benefits; there have also been serious reverses, however, as in Egypt when Sadat turned from Moscow to Washington.

The strategy of a "united front" is most effective during a revolutionary situation. It is therefore likely to be much used during the 1980s. Rather than working on their own or marching under the banner of communism, Marxist-Leninists like to work by means of militant fronts or liberation movements. Victory having been achieved through a "national democratic revolution," the party's "feudal" or "bourgeois" allies are then destroyed and their leaders suborned, jailed, hanged, or shot. The struggle for "scientific socialism" begins in earnest under the sole guidance of the new ruling party, whose functionaries in theory serve as the representatives of the proletariat and in practice form a self-appointed and newly privileged elite.

In Afghanistan the monarchy was toppled by a militantly Islamic movement led by Mohammed Daud, a relative of the former king and himself a former prime minister. The People's Democratic Party of Afghanistan, a small Marxist-Leninist body, initially joined Daud in a united front. According to the party's official account, "after the Daud coup [1973], we intensified our work in the armed force. Our party leadership had always given them much attention. The party had always schooled comrades wearing the uniform, had educated them politically and ideologically".[5] Daud was in turn overthrown by "the vanguard party of the working class," which set up a Marxist-Leninist dictatorship. Traditional Muslim villagers resisted gun in hand, but this time there was not even a pretense of relying on proxy troops; Soviet combat forces intervened directly, the first time they had done so openly in support of a Marxist regime outside Eastern Europe. Khomeini may expect similar treatment in Iran, unless he is careful.

According to the optimists in Washington, the Soviet invasion of Afghanistan in fact entailed a Soviet defeat. Public opinion in the United States hardened; former doves began to act like hawks. The United States imposed a grain boycott on the Soviet Union; Moscow lost credits and valuable equipment. The Soviet Union incurred bitter criticism in the United Nations. Bangladesh and Pakistan called for an emergency meeting of the Islamic Conference, which numbers Afghanistan among the forty-two members. Only South Yemen and some radical Palestinian groups gave support to the Soviet invasion. The Afghanistan venture also exacted a considerable military price from the Soviet Union; the occupying forces failed to set up a viable satellite government, and about one hundred thousand Soviet troops had to be deployed to contain popular unrest. Afghanistan, a rugged country peopled by rugged men and women, was supposed to become a "Soviet Vietnam."

A number of liberal-minded commentators took a somewhat different line. Moscow's gamble, they argued, was defensive in character. Spreading Islamic unrest would in fact involve the Soviet Union's own Muslim subjects. According to interpreters, such as veteran journalist Leo Gruliow, the Soviets also feared an American incursion into Iran, following the demise of the Iranian monarchy and the taking of US hostages. Another such explanation hinged on Soviet fears of China.

But the world is seen differently through the spectacles worn by the men in the Kremlin. They know that Afghan resistance is disunited; that the guerrillas derive their cohesion in the main from the links of clanship and lineage; that there is no cohesive political party that embraces the opposition as a whole. The guerrillas are poorly armed. They lack support from regular military forces, such as the massive armored formations that in the end won victory for the North Vietnamese in South Vietnam. Unlike the North Vietnamese, moreover, the Afghan guerrillas cannot rely on privileged sanctuaries; Pakistan knows better than to invite Soviet retaliation. The geographical contacts between China and Afghanistan, the tenuous and inhospitable mountain corridor, can easily be cut. Neither does the defensive argument make much sense. If the Soviets had been afraid of Muslim radicalism, they would hardly have given encouragement to Islamic radicals like Khomeini in Iran and the PLO gunmen in Palestine. The Russians are also well aware of their military advantage over the Americans. They are geographically nearer—they have to go only three hundred miles, the Americans seven thousand—they have more men and more equipment available locally, and they have better logistic facilities in the area. From a Soviet marshal's standpoint, the invasion demonstrated to the world the extent of Soviet might. The Afghanistan venture also had the additional advantage of providing combat experience to Soviet troops and of testing Soviet staff arrangements under difficult conditions—not to speak of such mundane rewards as medals and promotions for deserving members of the Red Army.

From the American standpoint, the Soviet invasion of Afghanistan constitutes a major defeat. For the first time since World War II, Soviet troops have directly intervened outside the Soviet Union's traditional sphere of influence, without even bothering to use proxy troops like the Cubans or the North Vietnamese. The invasion has given to the Soviet Union control of a strategic area that threatens Pakistan, Iran, and the Persian Gulf. Soviet air and land forces are now better placed than before to cut off Western oil supplies. The Soviets are able to put additional pressure on Pakistan and Iran. They may try to use the well-proven device of employing "liberation fronts" (coalitions of political opposition groups that include Communists). In Iran the Soviets might try to organize ethnic fronts among the Afghans, Baluchis, Kurds, Azerbaijanis, Arabs, and others. More use will certainly be made of communist groups like the Tudeh Party, which may try to form a united front to overthrow the present regime. Iran, at the moment, is a fragmented country, almost ungovernable. A number of ethnic groups are already in a state of revolt. Marxists and their allies may, at a later date, seize strategic cities and oil fields to form a new leftist government. Once in power, the front (as in South Yemen,

Ethiopia, and Afghanistan) will seek to eradicate the so-called nonprogressive elements and—if necessary—call on Soviet forces to render "fraternal help" against "imperialist" machinations on the part of Washington. The Soviets, it is reported, have begun to train and arm the Baluchis in order to establish a state of Baluchistan that would be carved out of Afghanistan, Pakistan, and Iran, and that would stretch all the way to the Indian Ocean.

We shall have to reconsider our relations with the various powers of the Indian subcontinent. Some analysts consider that we must at all costs strengthen Pakistan. They urge that we build up the Pakistani armed forces and turn Pakistan into an armed bastion, complete with US bases. The Pakistani regime, however, is weak, unstable, and beset with troubles. In any case, President Zia has rejected our aid. American backing, moreover, would entail worsening relations with India, the giant of the subcontinent. India's armed forces number over a million as against Pakistan's four hundred thousand. India's defense expenditures exceed Pakistan's by about four times; past fighting between India and Pakistan has proved the worth of India's armed forces and the efficiency of its new arms industries. It is India whom we should court, rather than Pakistan. If we are to restore our threatened position in the

FIGURE 5.2 BALUCHISTAN'S STRATEGIC SPOT ON THE INDIAN OCEAN

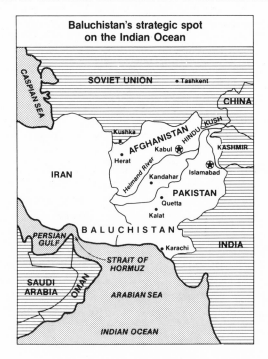

Indian Ocean, we must work for an Indo-American rapprochement, for it is New Delhi that holds the keys to the Indian Ocean.

The Soviet invasion of Afghanistan forms part of a wider strategic pattern. Soviet strategy in Afghanistan supplements the successes already attained by Soviet policy in South Yemen, another strategically situated country in the Middle East. In South Yemen, a National Front for the Liberation of Occupied South Yemen was formed in 1963, its avowed object to drive out the British. South Yemen achieved independence in 1967. The Marxist-Leninists within the ruling coalition then prepared, in their own words, "the necessary conditions for the transformation of the National Front into a vanguard party of the working class." They sought to achieve this object through intensifying the class struggle and through tightening their links with "the socialist community countries headed by the Soviet Union, and with other contingents of the world revolutionary movement." In 1978 the Marxist-Leninists took over and set up the Yemeni Socialist Party (YSP) as the sole repository of power.[6] Yemen became a military base for Cuban troops and for a powerful airborne force of mixed provenance capable of intervening anywhere in the area on short notice. South Yemen also turned into a sanctuary for guerrillas operating against Oman and North Yemen and was a supply point for Soviet naval units operating in the Indian Ocean. With Cuban instructors, Cuban pilots, and Soviet technicians, and equipped with the most modern arms, the "liberation" forces have become a formidable menace not merely to North Yemen and Oman but also to Saudi Arabia. Continued trouble can also be expected in the Horn of Africa until the Soviets and their proxies in Ethiopia are neutralized or countered.

Seen in a wider context, the Soviet Union and its allies enjoy a number of distinct advantages in the Middle East. Iranians and Turks have bitter memories of past Russian aggression, but the Soviet Union is remote from most Arab countries. The Arabs have experienced only the Western kind of imperialism, not that of the Soviets. Western investments remain popular targets of hostility. The West is widely censured both as an agent of modernization and as the putative cause of Middle Eastern backwardness. Western propaganda has failed to turn to good advantage the Soviets' own record as a colonial power in Central Asia, the Caucasus, and Eastern Europe, or the Soviet Union's hostility to Islam. The lack of a large, class-conscious Middle Eastern proletariat, far from weakening the communist cause, may actually serve it in countries where the working classes want nothing to do with communism but where the intellectuals are powerful as a group, and are widely influenced by Marxist notions. Above all, the West is associated with Israel, and Israel, for all its puny size, serves as the universal scapegoat for all the ills that beset the Arab world.

Fortunately for the West, Soviet policy in the Middle East has evinced serious weaknesses of its own. Between 1978 and 1979 the ruling Ba'athist Party, angered at the Iraqi Communist Party's antireligious stance and disconcerted at developments in Iran, put down the Iraqi Communists with a strong hand. Iraq increasingly turned to the West, especially to France, for the supply of new weapons. The country also improved its relations with Saudi Arabia.

The Soviets have to contend with numerous other obstacles. Unlike the regimes in Prague or East Berlin, the Middle Eastern governments are not creatures of the Kremlin, installed by foreign conquerors. Moreover, Islam remains a potent ideological force, one not easily harnessed to Soviet purposes. Economically, the Middle Eastern countries remain tied to the West, which supplies their principal markets and the bulk of their imports. Given a willingness on the part of these countries to use Western resources and Western strength to their best advantage, the ongoing battle for this region need not be lost, but we must take the ideological offensive against the Communists and their radical clients. We must provide military forces to shore up friendly regimes, even if these should not be models of democracy. We should take a leaf out of the Soviet book by supporting anti-Soviet guerrillas in Afghanistan and other Soviet dependencies by means of money, arms, and training; we should recognize such partisans as "freedom fighters" and massively support them in all international forums in which we are represented.

The ongoing battle for the region cannot, however, be won by the United States or the West alone. The West cannot simply solve the region's problems, whether military, economic, or political; indeed, the constant search for instant solutions has been a bane of US foreign policy. The United States cannot teach Arab governments how better to govern or how to improve the management of their resources. The United States can step in only when its help is requested and when it can operate with the assistance of such local allies as Israel or Egypt. The Palestinian question is too complex to be "solved" by means of a simple formula, even though it creates many of the problems that allow the Soviets to gain influence and burden the entire region with a wasteful and expensive arms race.

Faced with the Soviet offensive, the United States labors under many disadvantages. We Americans are the chief—indeed, the only—great foreign supporters of Israel. We are capitalistic and democratic. We own the major share of foreign investment in the Middle East. We have meddled in local politics and started the arms race in the area. In the eyes of our critics, we can do no right. If we invest abroad, we are guilty of exploiting foreign countries. If we do not invest, we incur blame for "boycotting" foreign economies. If we sell modern arms, we are responsible for profiting from the implements of war. If we do not sell up-to-date weapons, we are guilty of imperialist selectivity. The list of linked charges never ends. Americans have no instrument comparable to the communist parties' front groups or radical cliques that support Moscow.

These are well trained and disciplined; they are supported by enormous propaganda, intelligence, and military machines that command the resources of countries as varied as Cuba, the German Democratic Republic, and the Soviet Union, and they find fellow travelers in every Western nation.

The United States has been responsible for a series of grave tactical mistakes. It was foolish to stake all on the fate of a single ruler such as the former shah of Iran. To make matters worse, the US government actually encouraged the shah in great dreams of power that bore no relation to reality. Sophisticated military equipment poured into Iran as it now pours into Saudi Arabia. Yet the Iranian armed forces were not able to use or to maintain many of these weapons, which merely constituted a serious drain on local resources. Nor can Saudi Arabia be used as a policeman of the Persian Gulf. The Saudis cannot act as policemen anywhere outside their own borders; indeed, they could barely defend themselves on their own against a well-planned "war of liberation" supported by Cuban, Soviet, or East German experts. Given its military and economic deficiencies, even Egypt for the moment is hardly in a position to serve as a local proxy for the United States; Israeli forces are militarily efficient but for political reasons cannot be employed in the Arab world.

US policy, shaped by an endemic moralism and by ethnic pressure groups, has been equally successful in alienating Turkey, formerly America's strongest ally in the area. The Cyprus debacle has been followed by a rapprochement between Turkey and the radical Arab states in which Turkey has received financial aid and acquired new markets. The Western alliance is thus in a state of disarray throughout the Middle East. Conceivably, the West might have to contend during the 1980s with a radicalized Middle East controlled by anti-Western parties of a Marxist or militant Muslim type.

The "Vietnam syndrome"—fear of getting bogged down in an unpopular foreign war—has troubled the Carter administration. Watched carefully by Congress, it has hesitated to act decisively or to plan strategically. All too many politicians seem fearful of intervening anywhere in the world, no matter how important our interests are. Faith is put in diplomacy, not in military power, so Carter has been indecisive and weak. The War Powers Resolution of 1973 has severely restricted a president from sending troops to trouble spots; the gesture of sending unarmed F-15s to Saudi Arabia during the Yemen War of 1979 was typical. The presidency must reassert itself in the 1980s and stop Congress from playing special-interest politics with what should be a bipartisan foreign policy.

It is not as if we lacked advantages over our Soviet rivals in the area. Despite much overt hostility from intellectuals, we are generally better liked than are the Soviets; especially in Turkey, Iran, and Israel, and in conservative Arab states such as Saudi Arabia, we are widely seen as a necessary counterweight to communism. We have important economic assets; US goods are more valued. We have food surpluses in areas where food is scarce. American multinational corporations, no matter what leftists say, are good employers and efficient producers. American banks and financial institutions, corporations and businesses, goods and technology, give us clear advantages in the area if we can sell ourselves and our products. Technological superiority in agriculture, nuclear power, desalinization, solar energy, and computers is especially valuable in the Middle East. The first desideratum remains a stable peace treaty between Israel and Egypt with US guarantees for both signatories. The advantages of a treaty to the United States are manifold. Egypt and Israel alike are opposed to the communist camp. An end of hostilities between them would diminish the possibility of future Soviet intervention in the area.

A neutralized Palestinian state is not an ideal solution, but it is the best that can be hoped for. The state would be in no position to absorb the bulk of the Palestinian refugees now living in the remainder of the Arab world. It would, however, afford them a homeland; they could become citizens of a recognized country, hold recognized passports, and have a possible refuge.[7] "Middle Palestine," the land between Israel and Jordan, could play the same role for the Palestinian diaspora that Israel provides for world Jewry: a focus of national loyalty. At the same time, the United States should encourage other Arab states to provide full civil rights for those permanent immigrants of good standing who choose to stay. Hopefully, the conclusion of a peace treaty will split the united Arab front, ultimately persuading Iraq and Syria to recognize Israel.

The militant Palestinians are a major roadblock to peace in the Middle East. As long as Arab states support them there can be no settlement. The present treaty only takes Egypt out of the fight. These militants, then, have to be muzzled before they destroy any more states and before they provoke another *jihad* against Israel. Jordan was the first to war with them and drive them out; the Palestinian guerrillas then concentrated their efforts on Lebanon, which was cast into chaos. As a result of the Palestine problem, Middle Eastern states have wasted billions on armaments and fought three senseless wars. If the conservative states bordering on Israel were to withdraw support from the Palestinians, the Arab world would have a better chance of returning to stability.

A solution will be hard to find, for the Palestinians are as hardy and as resolute and as convinced of the absolute justice of their case as the Jews. They are exposed to constant discrimination in many Arab states; hence they are not at present being absorbed by other Arab peoples. PLO fighters are being trained in the Soviet Union and Eastern Europe and the USSR has come to regard the PLO as a valuable asset. The PLO supplies shock formations like the bodyguard of Idi Amin, former president of Uganda, intelligence agents and guerrillas capable of engaging in a variety of political and military operations that would not automatically implicate the USSR in their execution. The PLO has also become an intermediary for supplying arms to the so-called national liberation movements and other subversive organizations in other parts of the world. Even a truce with the PLO will be hard to achieve. Real peace will have to wait for the remote future when the grandchildren of the present refugees will hopefully have been absorbed into their respective countries of refuge.

Meanwhile the United States should withdraw financial support from Palestinian refugee camps in the Arab world. The existence of these camps, despite their ostensibly humanitarian purposes, prevents the Arab host governments from confronting the permanence of Palestinian exile. They delay the refugees' assimilation into their respective host countries. The camps become centers of Palestinian irredentism as well as abodes of misery and discontent. Moreover, such aid thrusts on the United States a burden that is not shouldered by the USSR or by the Arab countries themselves and that in no wise serves US interests.

The United States cannot easily operate in the Middle East without local allies. The Turkish alliance, as we have said, should be rebuilt if possible. In addition, the United States should continue to sustain both Israel and Egypt. But Americans would be unwise to overestimate the collective strength of even these two countries. The Western presence in the Middle East must be supported, therefore, by a combined effort on the part of the Western European countries, especially Great Britain and France. The departure of the British forces from east of Suez was a serious blow to American interests. Now the burden of containing the Soviet influence in the Middle East should be spread among the main oil users, including Japan.

This object might best be secured by extending the geographical field of NATO to the South Atlantic and the Western Indian Ocean, both of which are as vital to the alliance for strategic ports, harbors, airfields, and supply depots as for oil supply routes. The policy of furnishing desert states with vast arsenals of supermodern weapons should cease. Countries like Saudi Arabia lack the population to maintain large forces; they would do better to maintain small professional forces capable of dealing with guerrilla incursions and local policing problems rather than to import equipment that they cannot really use. We need to provide the Saudis and the gulf states with a protective umbrella such as the British provided until 1971. Forces capable of reacting quickly to threats must be developed by NATO, which needs to develop air transport and mobile elite military divisions that can fly anywhere in the Middle East to resist aggression. Given the divergence of aims within NATO, this strategy will not be easy to implement unless the caliber of American diplomacy improves and NATO's major European allies are accorded an important part in the decision-making process—a part that accords with their separate national interests as well as with the interests of the United States. If NATO will not act, then West Germany, Great Britain, France, and the United States should form a four-power group to intervene when the West's interests are endangered.

Saudi Arabia wants an air defense system. The United States can provide such a system from aircraft based in the Sinai at one of the bases Israel has left. Prepositioning material, and at least laying out the outlines of airfields, repair facilities, and supply depots, in Israel and in the Sinai, would do much to reassure Egypt and the Saudis and would remove the latter's fear of being attacked by the radical states or the Palestinians. Naval forces in the Persian Gulf area and off the Horn of Africa would also bolster the morale of conservative rulers. At the present time they fear the PLO and Soviet-sponsored liberation movements. If we can remove that fear the Saudis are less likely to stay in the radical camp and to isolate Egypt.

There is no question that this sustaining American influence will require more effort in the 1980s, for internal events in the developing countries will be difficult to control. We must learn to live with instability. Unsavory radical regimes are likely to take over from conservatives or from inept military regimes. Nevertheless, strong-arm tactics or CIA-orchestrated coups are simply not an answer any more; even if we had the will, we would not have the apparatus to carry out such operations. Rapid modernization and Marxist ideology are going to produce turbulence and revolution anyway. In such regions we will be handicapped in competing with the Soviet Union for the friendship of various successor governments. Accordingly, multinational forces provided by the West must protect Israel, Saudi Arabia, and the Persian Gulf. In addition, we should—if possible—help the Arabs form an effective Arab League force to counter revolution and invasion.

The United States must also seek to stabilize its currency. Inflation is a worldwide threat to prosperity. The United States has set a bad example to Third World countries in living beyond its means, subsisting on unbalanced budgets, and penalizing those of its citizens who are willing to save. By depreciating the value of the dollar, the United States may have contributed to the inflationary problems of countries like Iran that were paid for their exports in dollars of diminishing value.

Finally, the Western powers must be willing to take up the Soviets' ideological and military challenge. As long as the world's communist parties consider themselves at war with all other social systems, the West cannot and dare not avoid the challenge. Fortunately, the Soviet Union is itself highly vulnerable to ideological assaults carried out through broadcasts, television programs, diplomatic statements, and other such media of communications. The Western propaganda offensive, to be successful, should rest on three simple principles: propaganda must command the listeners' respect through a reputation for unvarnished factual accuracy, propaganda must be acceptable in content to its recipients; and ideological assaults, like military ones, should be directed against the opponents' points of maximum weakness. The contradictions within the Soviet system are plentiful. There are the contradictions between the Soviet hegemonic power and its minor allies; the contradictions between the great Russian nation—state and the Soviet nationalities (not merely the Jews); the contradictions between the communist Great Powers; the contradiction between the ruling class of party functionaries and ideologues on the one hand and the masses on the other; the contradiction between Marxism-Leninism and the great religions of mankind with which the Communists, for the sake of ultimate victory, now seek a "historic compromise." Whatever their tactical shifts and their internal differences, the communist parties in practice claim to be all-wise, all-powerful, and all-good. These claims are as incompatible with the precepts of Islam as they are with those of Judaism and Christianity. If the West will only take up the gauntlet, Marxism-Leninism cannot prevail.

In the short run, since we cannot reduce our dependence on oil from the area, we shall have to protect our supplies. This means arming. Furthermore we cannot avoid competition with the Soviets. The combination of peaceful coexistence and détente has not ended the struggle. We have to choose the best forms of competition, and to do this we shall need military strength. We shall have to practice *preventive diplomacy*, that is, diplomacy aimed at reducing Soviet opportunities and limiting potential conflict situations. Through diplomacy we can build a network of cooperation and alliances and thus a division of military responsibilities. Hopefully this will keep the peace and ensure our oil supplies at least through 1985. Meanwhile we have to search for new, more reliable sources of oil and, while practicing conservation, push ahead with new technologies for supplying energy through nuclear and solar energy, windpower and coal liquification.

A harsher, more perilous age lies ahead. We do not want to turn the United States into a garrison state, but we shall not survive as a democracy unless we rearm and show willingness to project our power where our vital interests are involved. We must replace rhetoric with resolve and détente with dynamic defense.

The search for an appropriate level of defense spending must not be sidetracked by either mirror-imaging of Soviet intentions or domestic pressure politics. As Air Marshall Sir John Slessor has written: "It is customary in democratic countries to deplore expenditures on armaments as conflicting with the requirements of the social services. There is a tendency to forget the most important social service that a government can provide for its people is to keep them alive and free."

EPILOGUE

In the fall of 1980 Governor Reagan was elected president and General Haig was nominated as secretary of state. The new administration faced a position even more difficult than its predecessor's. America's NATO allies in Europe were proving reluctant to shoulder new military responsibilities. The Soviet Union continued with its policy of expansion. As Sheikh Ahmed Zaki Yamani, Saudi Arabia's oil minister, described it, the war in the Horn of Africa, Soviet support for Ethiopia, the Soviet invasion of Afghanistan, and Soviet activities in South Yemen all pointed to the Soviet Union's major aim—command over the oil fields in the Middle East. Control of Middle East oil would enable the Soviet Union and its allies to guard against depletion of Soviet energy resources and to finlandize Western Europe and Japan by threatening to withhold all supplies, leaving the United States in a dangerous condition of political and military isolation.

While the West's attention centered on the gulf war and the question of the West Bank, the Soviets continued to strengthen their position in the Mediterranean. The Soviet involvement in Libya, though little noticed by the Western press, assumed critical importance. By 1980, the Soviets had established in Libya a massive military infrastructure, complete with air bases, military docking facilities, depots, and repair shops. Benghazi and Tripoli had become major Soviet naval bases. Soviet aircraft, painted with the Libyan colors but manned by North Korean or Soviet pilots, stood ready to attack the US Sixth Fleet in the Mediterranean. There were over three thousand North Koreans and six thousand Soviet advisers in Libya in 1980.

Military control in Libya had become a splendid substitute for the Soviet's lost position in Egypt—with far-reaching consequences for the Western naval position in the Mediterranean and the Middle East. By 1980, the Soviet Union had supplied Libya with the ultra-modern MiG-25-(Forbot) and the SS-22 missile, which has a range of over 650 miles and the ability to carry both conventional and nuclear warheads. The Soviets operated regular intelligence and surveillance flights in the eastern Mediterranean against NATO interests.

The Soviets had built up a huge reservoir of arms, including the most modern aircraft and over two thousand tanks. Together with the Soviet equipment in Algeria and Syria, the equipment and facilities in Libya helped to tip the balance in the Mediterranean in favor of the Soviets. Libya had become a refueling stop for Soviet cargo planes delivering equipment and supplies to Angola and Mozambique. Libya had become an intelligence base. In addition, Libya served as a staging base and ally in Soviet clandestine activities in Europe and the Middle East. Libya permitted the PLO to train with heavy weapons, including aircraft and tanks; Libyans and PLO members cooperated in Iran; and Libyan assassination squads murdered opponents of the Libyan regime in Europe. Finally, the Libyan alliance served the Soviet Union in the economic sphere. Libya paid for Soviet military assistance in oil, which the Soviet Union then sold in Western Europe in exchange for military and civilian technology.[1]

From the US standpoint, the wisest course against Libya would be to strengthen both Israel and Egypt, to reinforce the Sixth Fleet, and to support Israeli clandestine operations and other allied intelligence services against Libyan and PLO murder squads. Instead of merely looking to the defense of its allies, the United States should make more active use of its opponents' internal weaknesses. For instance, the United States should give massive support to the Eritrean guerrillas against Ethiopia; by doing so, Washington would both render Ethiopia more vulnerable and improve US relations with all those Arab states that support the Eritreans. Morocco should be used as a base to counter Soviet bases in Libya and Tunisia.

The Western position in relation to Iraq and Iran was no more encouraging at the end of 1980. The gulf war had reached a stalemate in which victory or peace seemed equally remote for either side. Iraq had gone to war to reverse an unfavorable settlement made under duress in 1975, when the shah had seemed at the height of his power and when Iraq had been on the defensive. The immediate cause of the war concerned the Iraqi-Iranian border along the Shatt al-Arab; the Iraqis had agreed to recognize the middle of the Shatt al-Arab as the border in return for the cessation of Iranian support for the Kurds. In September 1980 Saddam Hussein, Iraq's strong man, abrogated the agreement by claiming full control over the Shatt-al-Arab estuary and waterway, as well as additional frontier rectifications in approximately 670 places along the Iraqi-Iranian border. The Iraqis had designs moreover, on the Iranian province of Khuzistan (known to Arabs as Arabistan), which contains most of Iran's oil reserves and good deep-water ports. The large Arabic-speaking minority in Khuzistan has so far not supported the Iraqis.

Iraq, equipped with plenty of Soviet tanks, intended a swift assault when Iran seemed to have fallen apart and the Iranian forces appeared demoralized. From Iraq's point of view, war had far-reaching advantages. Victory would make Iraq the policeman of the Persian Gulf and Baghdad the dominant capital in the Middle East, vastly augment Iraq's oil wealth, and make it impossible for Iran to subvert Iraq through the latter's influential Shia community, which makes up about 55 percent of the population of a country essentially run by a Sunni minority. Victory over the Persians, the Arabs' age-old enemy, would make President Saddam Hussein, the Middle East's most prominent statesman, the new Saladdin, who might one day lead the Arabs to victory against Israel, supposedly a state of latter-day Western crusaders.

The gulf war had unsuspected diplomatic consequences. Iraq, though militarily equipped by the Soviet Union, had been moving away from the Moscow alliance; Iraqi communists had been subjected to brutal persecution. The gulf war brought about a striking realignment within the Arab world. Iraq, hitherto a capricious and violently radical force within the Arab world, won the support of Saudi Arabia, Jordan, and the conservative Arab gulf states, all of which had a common interest in opposing Khomeini's Shi'ite revolution. Iraq's defection from the radical ranks occasioned a major shift in the Middle Eastern balance of power. As long as Iraq adhered to the radical states—Syria, Libya, Algeria, and South Yemen—the PLO held the political initiative. The gulf war changed the balance of power. Syria and Libya, supporters of Iran, found themselves in a difficult position; Arab support for the PLO rapidly diminished; and Israel's position was unexpectedly strengthened diplomatically. Iraq turned more often to France for its military equipment; and the Western position improved unexpectedly in the Middle East.

Iraq found itself in a powerful diplomatic position. Militarily, however, the Iraqi experts had miscalculated. Designs for a swift mobile campaign collapsed. Foreign invasion helped to consolidate the Iranian revolution, as militant Muslims and professional soldiers alike rallied in defense of their country. Given the vast disparity between the populations of Iran and Iraq (38 million against 13 million, respectively), Iraq could not easily face a war of attrition whose main weight would be borne by private soldiers, many of whom were drawn from the ranks of discontented Shi'ites.

From the American standpoint, the most satisfactory outcome of the gulf war would be peace achieved quickly on the basis of the status quo. The United States has no interest in a decisive victory for either side. An Iraqi triumph would make Iraq the predominant state in the Middle East and would endanger Israel. If Iran were defeated, the Tudeh Party and its allies would gain increasing influence; and the Soviet Union might invoke existing treaty obligations, never abrogated by Moscow, to march into Iran for the sake of "protecting" its neighbor. Victory for Iran, however, would strengthen Shi'ite radicalism, threaten Persian Gulf states, and further weaken the Western position. An extended stalemate would have almost equally undesirable consequences. A lengthy war would interfere with Middle Eastern oil production, at a time when the Iranian oil output has greatly declined and the damage inflicted on Iranian and Iraqi oil installations alike has contributed to a new rise in oil prices. War, moreover, might spread to the adjoining oil-producing states or even interfere with the vital oil traffic through the Strait of Hormuz. As part of the US campaign for peace, Washington would be well advised to step up the propaganda campaign against the Soviet Union to persuade both combatants that the chief danger to their respective independence comes not from one another but from Moscow.

The realities of American self-interest in the Middle East unfortunately have been obscured by the Iranian hostage crisis, which is essentially a side issue amid much graver concerns. The American public's real or supposed proclivity for human interest stories, the sensation-seeking of the US media, and the skillful manipulative tactics of the Iranians and their allies succeeded in placing the hostage question at the center of the stage. Suddenly, the illegality of Iran's conduct was forgotten, and the United States permitted itself to be dragged into the dock before an international jury. The remedy is clear. In the future, the United States should refuse to negotiate with foreign states over hostages. Such a policy sounds harsh and insensitive, but it is in fact more humanitarian and more in accord with the United States' national interest than the present policy of permitting lawbreakers to set the terms of the international agenda. If Washington does not take a firm line in this matter, the United States will only encourage militants to seek further concessions by similar tactics, thereby placing more American diplomatists in jeopardy.

Employment in the US Foreign Service, like work in a mine shaft, a fire department, or the armed forces, has its risks as well as its rewards. These risks simply have to be accepted. To give some limited protection to its representatives abroad, however, the United States should pass legislation of the kind proposed at the end of 1980 by Senator Hayakawa. Hayakawa's proposed bill would permit Congress to declare as enemy aliens US residents who are citizens of foreign states that have offended against American diplomatists abroad. Such a law would permit the United States to take reprisals, which should have been taken much earlier in the hostage crises, against militant Iranian students and diplomatists.

The 1980s promises to be a harsh and unpromising decade. The old securities and the former certainties have gone. The very survival of the United States is now at stake. It behoves us to reexamine our position and to reshape our priorities to deal with the perils that threaten us. The stalled Iraqi-Iranian war gives the United States a chance to rebuild its power and prestige in the Middle East. While no Arab government appears publicly willing to allow full-fledged American bases within its territory, some are ready to provide facilities under Arab sovereignty. Arrangements to obtain security facilities in the Persian Gulf to protect local governments and the West's oil supplies seem possible.

The Iranian-Iraqi war and the Soviet invasion of Afghanistan have made Arab governments aware of their vulnerability and ready to accept some forms of direct, but discreet, American military buildup. The war was also valuable in splitting the "Steadfast Front." Moderate states like Jordan and Saudi Arabia are now willing to cooperate with the United States. Radical states such as Syria and Libya are discredited for supporting non-Arab Iran. The West also benefits because the PLO has been weakened and divided by the conflict. The Reagan administration therefore has a fresh opportunity to obtain military bases in the Middle East, but only if it pushes ahead on a settlement of the Arab-Israeli dispute and helps Saudi Arabia build an alliance system with the gulf states. The Saudis can become the dominant power in the Persian Gulf by using oil, money, and diplomacy, not guns. Pakistan can provide the troops, and the West can supply the arms.

NOTES

Chapter 1

1. William R. Polk, *The United States and the Arab World* (Cambridge, Mass.: Harvard University Press, 1975) is perhaps the best introduction.

2. For an excellent short survey, see Bernard Lewis, *The Arabs in History* (New York: Harper, 1969).

3. Wilfred Thesiger, *Arabian Sands* (New York: Dutton, 1959), p. 127.

4. Ibid., p. 12.

5. Gen. 4:4–5.

6. Lewis, *The Arabs in History*, p. 55.

7. For a general account, see John S. Badeau et al., *The Genius of Arab Civilization: Source of Renaissance* (New York: New York University Press, 1975).

8. Oleg Grabar, "Alhambra, Court of Lions," in Badeau et al., *The Genius of Arab Civilization*, p. 102.

9. Translated by Ar-Rihana. Cited by Mounah A. Khouri, "Literature," in Badeau et al., *The Genius of Arab Civilization*, p. 35.

10. H. R. Trevor Roper, "Ibn Khaldoun and the Decline of Barbary," in his *Historical Essays* (New York: Harper Torch Books, 1966), pp. 24–34.

11. Trevor Roper, "A Case of Co-existence: Christendom and the Turks," in *Historical Essays*, pp. 173–78.

12. Bernard Lewis, *The Emergence of Modern Turkey* (London: Oxford University Press, 1969), pp. 26–28.

13. Austen H. Layard, *Discoveries in the Ruins of Nineveh and Babylon* (London, 1853), p. 653, cited by Jacques Barzun and Henry F. Graff, *The Modern Researcher* (New York: Harcourt Brace and Company, 1957), p. 3.

14. Cited by Lewis, *The Emergence of Modern Turkey*, p. 130.

15. Ibid., p. 38.

16. For an excellent account, see Albert Hourani, *Arabic Thought in the Liberal Age, 1798–1939* (London: Oxford University Press, 1970), esp. pp. 341–43.

17. Elie Kedourie, *Nationalism in Asia and Africa* (New York: World Publishing Company, 1970), pp. 48, 64.

18. Lord Cromer, *Modern Egypt*, 2 vols. (London, 1908), 2:134–36. Cromer's condemnation of Islam contrasts with the encomium of Lord Lugard, another great African administrator, in *The Dual Mandate in British Tropical Africa* (Hamden, Conn.: Archon Books, 1965), p. 595.

19. For a summary of modern Muslim economic thought, see Muhammad Abdul-Rauf, *The Islamic Doctrine of Economics and Contemporary Economic Thought* (Washington, DC: American Enterprise Institute, 1979). For detailed discussion of leftist movements in today's Middle East, see Maxime Rodinson, *Marxism and the Muslim World*, trans. Michael Pallis (London: Zed Press, 1980). Other valuable introductory works are W. Montgomery Watt, *What is Islam?* (London: Longman and Librairie du Liban, 1980); and Albert Hourani, *Europe and the Middle East* (London: Macmillan, 1980).

Chapter 2

1. W. B. Fisher, "The Middle East and North Africa: An Introduction," in *The Middle East and North Africa, 1978–79* (London: Europa Publications, 1978), pp. 3–25.

2. Georges de Bouteiller, "Arabie Saoudite aujourd'hui et demain," *Défense nationale*, December 1978, p. 48.

3. See J. C. Hurewitz, ed., *Oil, the Arab-Israel Dispute and the Industrial World: Horizon of Crisis* (Boulder, Colo.: Westview Press, 1979).

4. Development plans have given priority to infrastructural improvements. These have absorbed between 20 and 30 percent of investments, followed by industries and mining with between 16 and 35 percent. Agriculture generally came third, absorbing between 15 and 25 percent.

5. Arthur Smithies, *The Economic Potential of the Arab Countries* (Santa Monica, Calif.: The Rand Corporation, 1978).

6. A. L. Udovitch, *The Middle East: Oil, Conflict and Hope—Critical Choices for Americans* (Lexington, Mass.: Lexington Books, 1976). See chapter 2, on which we have drawn heavily for this section.

7. John Waterbury and Ragaei El Mallakh, eds. *The Middle East in the Coming Decade: From Wellhead to Well-Being?* (New York: McGraw-Hill, 1978), pp. 101–39.

Chapter 3

1. Mervin F. Verbit, "The Political Character of Judaism and Islam: Some Comparisons," *Middle East Review* 9 (Winter 1978–79):32–37.

2. Between 1912 and 1944 the Muslim population increased from 589,177 to 1,061,-277, the Jewish population from 83,790 to 528,702, and the Christian population from 71,464 to 135,547.

3. Dwight James Simpson, "Israel after Thirty Years," *Current History*, January 1979, pp. 14–18.

4. Articles 9 and 6 of the Palestinian National Covenant (1968): *Al-Mīthāq Al-Watanī Al Filastīnī.*

5. For a detailed statement of the anti-Zionist case, see Alfred M. Lilienthal, *The Zionist Connection: What Price Peace?* (New York: Dodd, Mead and Co., 1978).

6. A Harris poll conducted between 1974 and 1975 concluded that pro-Arab opinions were held by only 5 percent of white Protestants, 9 percent of white Catholics, 11 percent of Hispanic Americans, and 12 percent of black Americans. See Seymour Martin Lipset and William Schneider, "Carter Versus Israel: What the Polls Reveal," *Commentary* 64, no. 5 (November 1977):27.

7. Cited in *FBIS* (Federal Broadcasting Information Service), 29 January 1979.

Chapter 4

1. See Sepehr Zahib, *Iran's Revolutionary Upheaval: An Interpretative Essay* (San Francisco: Alchemy Books, 1979), pp. 68–71.

2. See John Kelly, "Saudi Arabia and the Gulf States," in *The Middle East: Oil, Conflict and Hope*, ed. A. L. Udovitch (Lexington, Mass.: Lexington Books, 1976), pp. 427–62—a masterful survey. See also Robert Graham, *Iran: The Illusion of Power* (London: Croom Helm, 1979).

3. See John K. Cooley, "Iran, the Palestinians and the Gulf," *Foreign Affairs*, Summer 1979, pp. 1017–34. See also John Kelly, "The Kremlin and the Gulf," *Encounter* 54, no. 4 (April 1980):84–90.

4. Joseph Szyliowicz, "Prospects for Scientific and Technological Development in Saudi Arabia," *International Journal of Middle East Studies* 2, no. 3 (August 1979): 355–72.

Chapter 5

1. Ragaei El Mallakh, "Oil and Energy Alternatives in the 1980s," in Waterbury and El Mallakh, eds., *The Middle East in the Coming Decade*, p. 153.

2. David E. Long, "The United States and the Persian Gulf," *Current History*, January 1979, p. 29.

3. For a brilliantly argued case against American military intervention, see James H. Noyes, *Persian Gulf Security and US Policy* (Stanford, Calif.: Hoover Institution Press, 1979). Noyes attempts to meet the arguments of interventionists such as Robert Tucker, Edward Friedlander, Aaron Wildavsky, and Paul Seabury. We believe, however, that with adequate preparation the technical obstacles to armed intervention can be solved.

4. Ferenc A. Vali, *The Turkish Straits and NATO* (Stanford, Calif.: Hoover Institution Press, 1972), p. 69.

5. Comments on the April 1978 revolution by Saleh Mohammad Zaray, Central Committee Political Bureau member of the People's Democratic Party of Afghanistan, *World Marxist Review* 22, no. 1 (January 1979):106.

6. Abdel Fattah Ismail, general secretary, Central Committee Yemeni Socialist Party, "A New Vanguard Party," *World Marxist Review* 22, no. 1 (January 1977):19–29.

7. Interview with Egyptian foreign secretary Butros Ghali, *Der Spiegel*, 8 January 1979, p. 88.

Epilogue

1. Yossef Bodansky, "Soviet Military Presence in Libya," *Armed Forces Journal*, November 1980, p. 89–93.

SUGGESTED READINGS

Antonius, George. *The Arab Awakening: The Story of the Arab National Movement*. Philadelphia: Lippincott, 1939.

Badeau, John S., ed. *The Genius of Arab Civilization: Source of Renaissance*. New York: New York University Press, 1975.

Graham, Robert. *Iran: The Illusion of Power*. London: Croom Helm, 1978.

Hourani, Albert. *Arabic Thought in the Liberal Age, 1789–1939*. London: Oxford University Press, 1967.

————. *Europe and the Middle East*. London: Macmillan, 1979.

Institute for the Study of Conflict. *The Security of Middle East Oil: An Assessment by an ISC Study Group of Destabilising Events in the World's Major Oil-Producing Area*. London: The Institute, 1979.

Issawi, Charles, ed. *The Economic History of the Middle East, 1800–1914: A Book of Readings*. Chicago: Chicago University Press, 1966.

Jansen, G. H. *Militant Islam*. London: Pan Books, 1979.

Kelly, John. *Arabia, the Gulf and the West*. London: Weidenfeld and Nicolson, 1980.

Knapp, Wilfred. *North West Africa: A Political and Economic Survey*. Oxford: Oxford University Press, 1977.

Laqueur, Walter. *The Struggle for the Middle East: The Soviet Union and the Middle East, 1958–70*. Harmondsworth, England: Penguin Books, 1972.

Legum, Colin, and Shaked, Haim, eds. *Arab Relations in the Middle East: The Road to Realignment*. New York: Holmes and Meier, 1978.

Lenczowski, George. *The Middle East in World Affairs*. 4th ed. Ithaca, NY: Cornell University Press, 1980.

Lewis, Bernard. *The Arabs in History*. London: Hutchinson, 1962.

————. *The Emergence of Modern Turkey*. London: Oxford University Press, 1978.

————. *The Middle East and the West*. Bloomington: Indiana University Press, 1964.

Mansfield, Peter, ed. *The Middle East: A Political and Economic Survey*. London: Oxford University Press, 1973.

Middle East Contemporary Survey. Edited by Colin Legum and Haim Shaked. Annual. New York: Holmes and Meier, 1980.

Noyes, James H. *The Clouded Lens: Persian Gulf Security and US Policy*. Stanford, Calif.: Hoover Institution Press, 1979.

Patai, Raphael. *The Arab Mind*. New York: Charles Scribner's Sons, 1976.

Peretz, Don. *The Government and Politics of Israel*. Boulder, Colo.: Westview Press, 1979.

Polk, William Roe. *The United States and the Arab World*. Cambridge, Mass.: Harvard University Press, 1975.

————. *The Elusive Peace: The Middle East in the Twentieth Century*. New York: St. Martin's, 1979.

Ro'i, Yaacov, ed. *The Limits to Power: Soviet Policy in the Middle East*. New York: St. Martin's Press, 1979.

Rostow, Eugene, ed. *The Middle East: Critical Choices for the US*. Westview Studies on the Middle East. Boulder, Colo.: Westview Press, 1976.

Sachar, Howard M. *A History of Israel: From the Rise of Zionism to Our Time*. Oxford: Basil Blackwell, 1977.

Saikal, Amin. *The Rise and Fall of the Shah*. Princeton, NJ: Princeton University Press, 1980.

Smith, Wilfrid Cantwell. *Islam in Modern History*. Princeton, NJ: Princeton University Press, 1957.

Smithies, Arthur. *The Economic Potential of the Arab Countries: Prepared for Director of Net Assessment, Office of the Secretary of Defense*. Santa Monica, Calif.: Rand Corporation, 1978.

Udovitch, A. L. *The Middle East: Oil, Conflict and Hope—Critical Choices for Americans*. Lexington, Mass.: Lexington Books, 1976.

Waterbury, John, and El Mallakh, Ragaei, eds. *The Middle East in the Coming Decade: From Wellhead to Well-Being*. New York: McGraw-Hill, 1978.

Watt, W. Montgomery. *What is Islam?* 2d ed. London: Longman, 1979.

Wilson, Rodney. *The Economies of the Middle East*. New York: Holmes and Meier, 1979.

INDEX